Getting Skills Right:
South Africa

This work is published under the responsibility of the Secretary-General of the OECD. The opinions expressed and arguments employed herein do not necessarily reflect the official views of OECD member countries.

This document and any map included herein are without prejudice to the status of or sovereignty over any territory, to the delimitation of international frontiers and boundaries and to the name of any territory, city or area.

Please cite this publication as:
OECD (2017), *Getting Skills Right: South Africa*, OECD Publishing, Paris.
http://dx.doi.org/10.1787/9789264278745-en

ISBN 978-92-64-27873-8 (print)
ISBN 978-92-64-27874-5 (PDF)

Series: Getting Skills Right
ISSN 2520-6117 (print)
ISSN 2520-6125 (online)

The statistical data for Israel are supplied by and under the responsibility of the relevant Israeli authorities. The use of such data by the OECD is without prejudice to the status of the Golan Heights, East Jerusalem and Israeli settlements in the West Bank under the terms of international law.

Photo credits: Cover © Cell phone: © Creative Commons/Alfredo Hernandez, clock: © Creative Commons/Hakan Yalcin, cloud upload: Creative Commons/Warslab, join: © Creative Commons/Tom Ingebretsen, doctor: © Creative Commons/Joseph Wilson, chef: © Creative Commons/Alfonso Melolontha.

Corrigenda to OECD publications may be found on line at: *www.oecd.org/about/publishing/corrigenda.htm.*

Foreword

Across countries, tackling skill mismatch and skill shortages is a major challenge for labour market and training policies in the context of rapid and substantial changes in skill needs. In most countries, a substantial share of employers complain that they cannot find workers with the skills that their businesses require. At the same time, many college graduates face difficulties in finding job opportunities matching their qualifications.

In light of this challenge, OECD has undertaken an ambitious programme of work on how to achieve a better alignment or skill supply and skill demand, with a focus on: i) understanding how countries collect and use information on skill needs; ii) investigating cost-effective training and labour market policies to tackle skill mismatch and shortages; iii) studying the incentives of training providers and participants to respond to changing skill needs; and iv) setting up a database of skill needs indicators.

This works builds on the extensive programme of work of the OECD in the area of skills, including the OECD Skill Strategy and its follow up national implementation strategies, the Survey of Adult Skills (PIAAC) and its rich analyses in the areas of skills mismatch, vocational education and training and work-based learning.

This policy review is one of a series on skill imbalances aiming to identify international best practice in addressing skill imbalances in order to minimise the associated costs to individuals, enterprises and economies. The review involves an in-depth assessment of the country's skills system, leading to a set of policy recommendations backed by analysis and input from country stakeholders.

The work on this report was carried out by Marieke Vandeweyer from the Skills and Employability Division of the Directorate for Employment, Labour and Social Affairs under the supervision of Glenda Quintini (team manager on skills) and Mark Keese (Head of the Skills and Employability Division). The report has benefited from helpful comments provided by Stefano Scarpetta (Director for Employment, Labour and Social Affairs) and staff at the JP Morgan Chase Foundation.

This report was produced with the financial assistance of the JP Morgan Chase Foundation. However, the views expressed in this report should not be taken to reflect the official position of the JP Morgan Chase Foundation.

Table of contents

Figures

Table

Acronyms and abbreviations

ABET	Adult Basic Education and Training
ATR	Annual training report
CHIETA	Chemical Industries SETA
CWP	Community Works Programme
DHET	Department for Higher Education and Training
EPWP	Expanded Public Works programme
EU	European Union
FET	Further Education and Training
GDP	Gross Domestic Product
HRDSA	Human Resource Development Strategy
ICT	Information and Communication Technology
ILO	International Labour Organisation
JIPSA	Joint Initiative on Priority Skills Acquisition
LMIP	Labour Market Intelligence Partnership
MAC	Migration Advisory Committee
MERSETA	Manufacturing Engineering and Related Services SETA
NCAP	National Career Advice Portal
NEET	Not in employment, education or training
NGO	Non-governmental organisation
NQF	National Qualifications Framework
NSDS	National Skills Development Strategy
NSF	National Skills Fund
NSFAS	National Student Financial Scheme
OFO	Organising Framework for Occupations
PES	Public Employment Service
PIVOTAL	Professional, vocational, technical and academic
PPP	Purchasing Power Parity
QCTO	Quality Council for Trades and Occupations

R&D	Research and Development
RPL	Recognition of Prior Learning
SAQA	South African Qualifications Authority
SETA	Sector Education and Training Authorities
SIP	Strategic Integrated Project
SME	Small and medium-sized enterprises
SSP	Sector Skills Plans
TEFSA	Tertiary Education Fund of South Africa
TIMSS	Trends in International Mathematics and Science Scores
TVET	Technical and Vocational Education and Training
UNESCO	United Nations Educational, Scientific and Cultural
WISE	World Indicators of Skills and Employment
WSP	Workplace Skill Plans
WTO	World Trade Organisation

Executive summary

As one of the world's largest emerging economies, South Africa's economy has seen significant improvements in recent decades. The economic composition of the country's output has been changing rapidly, moving away from resource-based industries and the manufacturing sector, towards a larger service sector. In this context, the existing stock of skills and its mobilisation into the labour market represent important bottlenecks for the country's further development. Educational attainment has increased substantially over the years but a large share of South Africans still leave the education system before finishing upper secondary education. Furthermore, South African students in secondary education perform poorly on international tests, suggesting that the quality of initial education is low. Educational outcomes are strongly dependent on socio-economic factors, with students from disadvantaged backgrounds at most risk of attending low quality schools and dropping out from secondary education. As a result of large gaps in education and labour market outcomes, South Africa has one of the highest levels of income inequality.

In addition to having a relatively small share of high-skilled individuals, high unemployment, inactivity and informality further reduce the effective use of the pool of skills available and their development through further training. The labour market is characterised by persistently high unemployment and low participation rates, affecting mainly youth, low skilled and individuals from disadvantaged backgrounds. The unemployed and inactive represent a pool of unused skills, which are at risk of obsolescence and depreciation. A substantial share of employment is in the informal economy, where the quality of jobs is generally lower and access to training limited.

Especially in the context of limited public resources, South Africa needs to invest in the right skills not just more skills in order to strengthen its economic and social development. In an era of fast-changing skills demand, driven by the further development of the South African economy and by global trends such as technological progress and globalisation, it is important to understand the skill needs of the country. Multiple skills assessment and anticipation exercises have been put in place in South Africa, and the system is undergoing continuous development. This skill needs information is used for career advice, the distribution of training funds, and the allocation of work visas. It will be crucial for South Africa to further develop its skill needs assessment and anticipation exercises, by making them less reliant on low-quality employer data, and to distribute the information more broadly to relevant stakeholders and the wider public.

South Africa has put a range of policies in place to tackle existing skills imbalances, and the importance of skills has been reflected in a number of development plans and strategies. In order to encourage individuals to invest in skills, the government has set up a loan and bursary system for post-school education and training, created a Nation Skills Fund to invest in specific skill development programmes and put in place alternative skills acquisition and recognition tools for individuals without formal qualifications. To better steer skills development, a career advice systems has been developed that should provide students, unemployed and employed individuals with information on available education and training options and whether these options will lead to employment in occupations that are in high demand. Employers are encouraged to provide workplace training through a skills development levy system and tax incentives for hiring learners. Job creation policies have been put in place to provide work experience for the unemployed, which will increase their overall employability. Finally, when the national education and training system is unable to supply the necessary skills to respond to demand, the influx of non-nationals with the required skills is facilitated through the introduction of a Critical Skills Visa.

Notwithstanding the efforts of the South African Government and a range of private sector stakeholders to tackle skills imbalances, some challenges remain. The educational system could be further improved, in terms of developing both basic skills and technical skills, with a specific focus on historically disadvantaged individuals. More training options are needed for the employed and the unemployed, and this training should be relevant for improving the employability and career progress of participants. Several governance aspects need to be addressed as well. A lack of co-ordination and co-operation between relevant stakeholders, such as government departments, training institutions and employers, hinders the development of effective skills policies and their implementation. The implementation of policies is often impeded by a lack of clear goals, a missing or underdeveloped monitoring and evaluation framework, and the instability of policy development.

The main recommendations for better addressing skills imbalances in South Africa are listed in the box below, and more detailed recommendations are provided in Chapter 4. These recommendations mainly focus on improving the quality and labour market relevance of investments in skills development. But they would need to be implemented together with other policies to shape more broadly the demand for and use of skills. These complementary policies go beyond the scope of this report but include policies to foster greater job creation and regional development.

Key recommendations

Skill needs information

- Develop a uniform method for Sector Education and Training Authorities (SETA) to identify skill needs. Provide training and support to SETAs who lack the capacity to implement this method. Alternatively, the skill needs assessment exercises could be centralised and executed by a body with strong statistical capacity.

- Rather than relying on the information from the Workplace Skill Plans (WSP), narrowly-defined and easily measurable employer information on (hard-to-fill) vacancies should be used. This information could be collected through a survey of a representative sample of firms. In order not to overburden employers, relevant questions could be added to an already existing employer survey, such as the Quarterly Employment Survey.

- The list of occupations in high demand produced by the Department for Higher Education and Training (DHET) should be distributed widely to all relevant stakeholders. To facilitate the use of the list, a dedicated webpage could be set up, which is user-friendly and provides more information on the shortage occupations. Following the example of the National Career Advice Portal (NCAP), the webpage should have an easy search function and occupations should have links to the required qualifications, as well as to available job openings (through the Public Employment Service). This webpage should be easy to find, and other relevant government departments or agencies, such as the Public Employment Service (PES), should refer to it.

Key recommendations *(cont.)*

Quality of education

- Encourage students to choose teaching as a career, by making the teaching profession more attractive. At the same time, increase the quality of teacher training. Provide additional incentives for teachers to teach in historically disadvantaged schools.

- Provide tailored career advice to students early on in the schooling system to reduce dropout, increase throughput to further education and improve labour market outcomes. As South African students make important subject choices at young ages, it is important for them to be well-informed about possible career paths. Career counselling should be an integral part of teacher training. Moreover, advice should be linked to each student's abilities, which should be assessed thoroughly before students make subject choices that influence their further study path. A re-introduction of a standardised test at the end of general education could be considered. Particular attention should be given to science and math subjects.

- Ensure sufficient and effective government spending on education. Private sector players should be encouraged to develop education funding initiatives both at the school and post-school level.

- Assure quality of education through regular school and class inspections, including teacher evaluations. Additionally, quality can be monitored through standardised tests.

Work-based and lifelong learning

- Better align the vocational education system to workplace practices and skill needs in the workplace. Teachers should be involved in continuous training to keep their skills up to date. The training offer and content should be responsive to local needs, and employers should be involved in every step of the TVET value chain. Vocational programmes should not be too specific to give graduates access to a wide range of employment opportunities.

- Employers should provide more workplace training opportunities for vocational students and existing employees. By reducing the administrative burden for firms, especially SMEs, on applying for funding under the skills development levy system, more firms could be willing to offer training. Employers providing workplace training should assign trained mentors to learners. Further promoting the learnership tax incentive could also increase the number of training places. Additional tax incentives or subsidies could be made available for SMEs.

- Promote the Recognition of Prior Learning (RPL) among employees and employers, as well as the unemployed. Make sure the mode of assessment is flexible, such that is tailored to the specific situation of the individual. Ensure that employees are supported by their employer during the process, e.g. in terms of time to work on their skills portfolio. PES workers should actively recommend RPL to the unemployed, and should provide assistance throughout the recognition process. RPL could go beyond hard skills and formal qualifications, and also recognise soft skills that are valued by employers.

- Scale up existing measures for training of the unemployed. Both SETAs and the National Skills Fund (NSF) should allocate sufficient resources to the unemployed, and the funds should prioritise training for skills in high demand. Not only should the PES provide information on training, but they could become a one-stop-shop where unemployed can register for training that suits their needs. As such, the PES should work closely with the SETAs, the NSF and community colleges, but also with private sector training providers (e.g. NGOs). These PES services should not be restricted to unemployed individuals eligible for benefits, as this tends to excludes first-time job seekers and re-entrants such as youth and women.

Co-ordination between stakeholders

- Improve co-operation across government departments. Strategies and policies should involve all relevant departments sharing efforts to reach agreed targets. Co-ownership of strategies and policies should be encouraged. Co-ordination with other departments should happen at an early stage.

<h2 style="text-align:center;">Key recommendations (cont.)</h2>

- Employers should be given the opportunity to voice their ideas and concerns on skills policies to policy makers, ideally through existing bodies like SETAs or employer organisations. The input from employers should be taken on board early in the policy development process. Trust between employers and government should be improved.

- The relationship between employers and training providers should be strengthened and improved, possibly by strengthening the role of the SETAs as intermediaries and by creating platforms for co-operation. This will give a chance to employers to communicate directly with training providers on local skill needs. By creating close links with employers, training institutions would find it easier to accommodate demand for workplace learning.

Policy implementation

- Set measurable targets in strategic documents in order to facilitate monitoring and evaluation. These targets should be based on research, and should be set at ambitious but not unrealistic levels. To ensure engagement in reaching the targets, stakeholders should be actively involved in the target-setting process. Overall, stakeholders should be involved during each step of policy making in order to provide a sense of ownership

- Ensure that policies and strategies are not too sensitive to the political cycle. Well-designed policies and strategies should not disappear or be changed dramatically every time there is a change of minister or government.

- Evaluate the measures put in place to ensure that they are delivering the intended results in a cost-effective way. Robust evaluations using experimental methods should be privileged where possible and applicable when introducing new policies.

Chapter 1

Key drivers of skills demand and supply in South Africa

Skills imbalances are driven by structural and cyclical factors that shape the demand for and supply of skills. For instance, economic growth, changes in the composition of economic output over time and the so-called mega-trends are all important macroeconomic factors influencing the demand for skills. On the other hand, labour market trends, migration, and skills and education outcomes play an important role in defining the supply of skills. The main drivers of skills demand and supply in South Africa are discussed in this chapter, together with the current state of skills imbalances.

The statistical data for Israel are supplied by and under the responsibility of the relevant Israeli authorities. The use of such data by the OECD is without prejudice to the status of the Golan Heights, East Jerusalem and Israeli settlements in the West Bank under the terms of international law.

Key economic trends and facts

Trends in South Africa's GDP growth, changes in the composition of its economic output over time, as well as differences from OECD and other upper-middle income countries are important factors behind the demand for skills in the country. Overall economic growth will strongly influence labour demand, and changes in the composition of the economy will determine the skills that are needed.

South Africa is one of the world's largest emerging economies. Real GDP growth in South Africa in the period 1995-2015 outpaced the growth rate in OECD countries, but remained below the even higher rates of growth recorded in other upper middle income countries (Figure 1.1). While the South African economy was hit less strongly by the global financial crisis than the average OECD country, it did experience negative GDP growth in 2009, and growth rates have not returned to their pre-crisis levels. South African growth has been modest compared to other upper middle income countries, especial since the early 2000s.

Figure 1.1. GDP volume growth, South Africa and OECD, 1995-2015

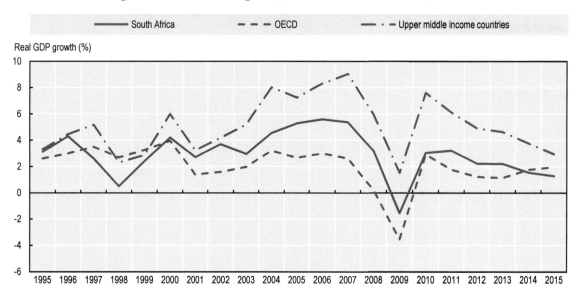

Source: OECD National Accounts Database, World Bank National Accounts Database.

Despite recording growth above the OECD average over the past two decades, GDP per capita in South Africa remains far below the level observed in OECD countries (Figure 1.2). Moreover, South Africa's level of GDP per capita has not shown any signs of convergence towards the OECD level and has grown more slowly than the average for upper-middle income countries. There are also large regional differences. GDP per head in the capital region, Gauteng, is more than twice the level in the poorest provinces (Eastern Cape and Limpopo).

Figure 1.2. GDP per capita, South Africa and OECD, 1995-2015

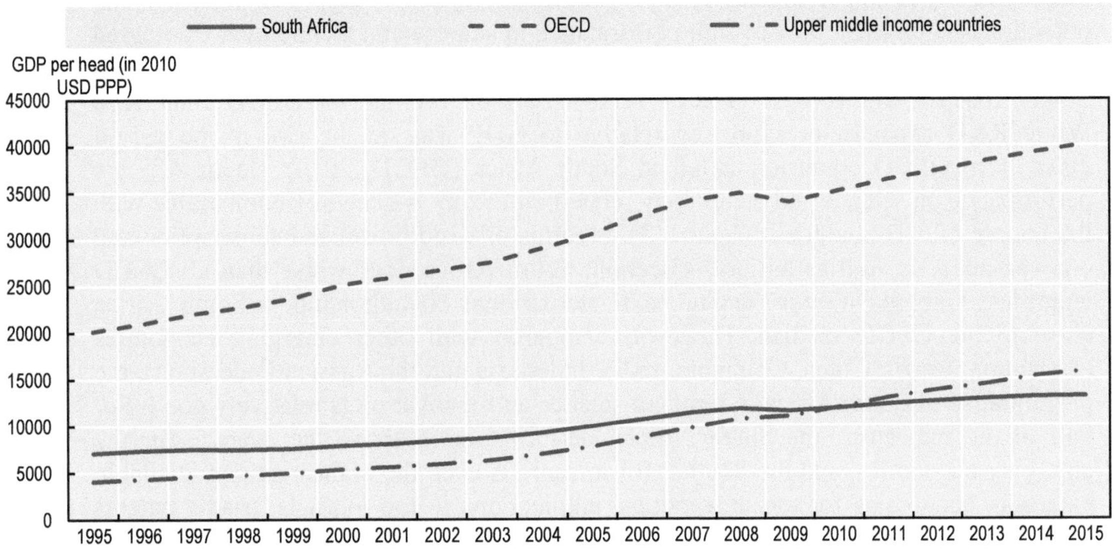

Source: OECD National Accounts Database, World Bank National Accounts Database.

The composition of South Africa's economic output differs from most OECD countries, and important changes have occurred over the last decades. Compared with OECD countries, South Africa has a large primary sector. While the share of agriculture, forestry and fishing in GDP in South Africa is similar to most OECD countries, the share of mining and quarrying is substantially bigger and increased from 7.1% of GDP in 1994 to 8.4% in 2014. However, this modest increase in the contribution of mining to GDP follows a prolonged period of decline from around 21% in 1970 (Fedderke and Pirouz, 2002). As in most OECD countries, the manufacturing sector has also been declining. While it represented 21% of GDP in 1994, this share dropped to 13.5% by 2014. Consequently, the Finance, Real Estate and Business Services sector accounted for the largest share of GDP in 2014 (20.2% compared to 15% in 1994).

South Africa is a relatively open economy, with exports representing 31% of GDP in 2014 and imports 33%. Exports and imports are dominated by merchandise trade, with commercial services representing only 15.3% of exports in 2014 and 12% of imports. While goods represent the biggest share of trade in most countries, their contribution is larger in South Africa than in European countries (70% of exports in EU-28 compared with 84.7% in South Africa, 75% of imports in EU-28, compared with 88% in South Africa). As in European countries, the largest share of South African imports and exports comes from the manufacturing sector. However, the manufacturing share of merchandise exports in South Africa is significantly smaller than in the EU-28 (46.5% compared to 79%). This is the result of South Africa's large mining sector, which represents 34.8% of exports. Compared to EU countries, South Africa also exports a relatively large share of agricultural products (12.5% compared to 7.9% in EU-28). Service exports in South Africa are dominated by travel, whereas the largest share of service imports is transportation-related (WTO Statistics Database).

A mixed picture emerges from indicators of the demand for higher-level skills. Only 5.9% of South Africa's manufactured exports have high R&D intensity

(UN Comtrade Database). This is very low compared to countries with similar income levels (20.6% in upper middle income countries). This low high-tech intensity can potentially be linked to low overall performance in science and technology. Compared with OECD countries, gross domestic expenditure on R&D as a proportion of GDP in South Africa is low (0.76% in 2014 versus 2.4% on average for OECD countries). While R&D expenditure expressed relative to GDP was on the rise in the period 2007-11 in OECD countries, it fell in South Africa (OECD, 2014). South Africa's performance on science and technology related indicators is generally comparable with the bottom OECD countries (Figure 1.3). In terms of fixed broadband subscription and e-governance, as well as tertiary education, South Africa does worse than all OECD countries. Only for venture capital and international co-authorship is South Africa close to the OECD median. However, compared with other emerging economies (Argentina, Brazil, China, Colombia, India, Indonesia and the Russian Federation), the performance of South Africa in terms of science and innovation is relatively good. For half of the indicators, the South African performance is above the average for the emerging economies, and the South African score is even the highest among available emerging economies for top universities, publications in top journals, triadic patents and patents filed by universities and public labs. Only for tertiary-education expenditure is South Africa the lowest performing emerging economy. The most recent Global Competitiveness Report (World Economic Forum, 2016) confirms that South Africa scores well in terms of innovation compared to countries at similar stages of development, but that its remains below most OECD countries.

Figure 1.3. Comparative performance of national science and innovation systems, South Africa and OECD, 2014

Normalised index of performance relative to the median values in the OECD area (Index median = 100)

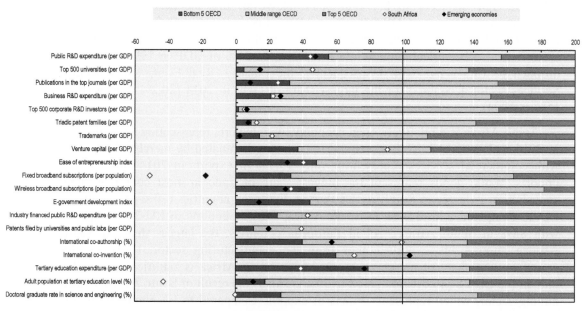

Note: Emerging economies is the unweighted average of the emerging economies with available data. Emerging economies are Argentina, Brazil, China, Colombia, India, Indonesia, Russian Federation and South Africa.

Source: OECD (2014).

Key labour market and social trends and facts

South Africa has been plagued by high unemployment rates, representing a substantial unused resource of skills at risk of obsolescence and depreciation. At 26.2% in the fourth quarter of 2016, South Africa is among the countries with the highest unemployment rate in the world. In the OECD, only Greece and Spain have unemployment rates above 20%, and the average across OECD countries was only 6.8% in 2015. In contrast to countries like Spain and Greece, South Africa's high unemployment rate is not just a recent phenomenon related to the recent global financial crisis: it has fluctuated around 25% during the last 25 years, with only a short period of lower unemployment in the mid-nineties (Figure 1.4). While unemployment was on the decline in the years before the start of the global financial crisis, it has been on the rise ever since. Recent estimates, however, suggest that the unemployment rate will decline modestly in 2017 (OECD, 2016). In 2015, 56% of the South African unemployed had been unemployed for 12 months or more. This incidence of long-term unemployment is much higher than the OECD average of 33.8%. Despite the strong increase in the South African incidence of long-term unemployment following the crisis (+9.6 percentage points between 2009 and 2011), the incidence remains below the level observed at the start of the century (68.4%) and has been declining slowly since 2012.

Figure 1.4. Unemployment rate, South Africa and OECD, 1990-2015

Unemployment rate (% of total labour force)

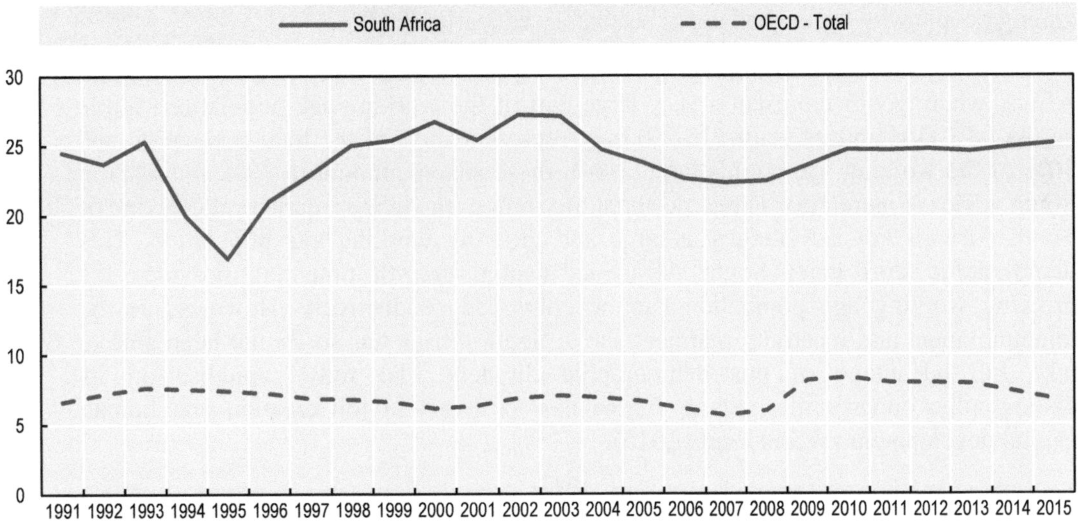

Source: *OECD Employment Database*; World Bank.

At the same time, labour market participation in South Africa is low. In 2015 the participation rate among individuals aged 15 to 64 in South Africa was 58.5%, compared with 71.2% across OECD countries and 72.5% among upper-middle income countries World Bank World Development Indicators, 2014). Among South African women, the participation rate was only 52%. The low participation rate is linked to high numbers of discouraged workers, i.e. persons who wanted to work but did not try to find work or start a business because they believed that there were no jobs available in their area, or were unable to find jobs requiring their skills, or they had lost hope of finding any kind of work. The share of discouraged workers reached 6.5% in South Africa in 2015 (Statistics South Africa, 2016), compared to only 0.5% across OECD countries in 2013.

The labour market picture is even worse when focussing on youth (15-24), whose unemployment rate in 2014 equalled 51.3% (compared with an OECD average of 15.1%). Although South Africa's high youth unemployment rate has been a persistent problem in the past decades, the rate increased significantly since 2008 (from 45.6%). Unemployment is higher among female youth (55.3%) than among male youth (48%). In addition to a large group of unemployed youth, South Africa also has a substantial share of discouraged youth, who exited the labour market because they lost hope of finding a job. This share of discouraged youth increased from 4.2% in 2008 to 7.6% in 2015 (Statistics South Africa, 2015a, 2016).

The share of young people neither employed nor in education or training (NEETs) provides an additional measure of youth people's idleness and social exclusion. In South Africa the share of NEETs among persons aged 15-29 was around 36% in 2015, compared with an OECD average of 14.6% (OECD, 2016). The share even increases to over 50% when focussing on 22-24 year-olds. South African woman are 5.4 percentage points more likely to be NEET than men (Statistics South Africa, 2016). Focussing on the group of 20-24 year-olds, the NEET rate decreases substantially with educational attainment, ranging from 74% among people without any schooling to 44.7% for people with upper secondary education (grade 12, also referred to as Matric in South Africa). Obtaining the secondary diploma significantly reduces the NEET probability, as the NEET rate among youth with lower secondary education reaches 60.7% and among people with unfinished upper secondary education 50.9%.

Ensuring good labour market outcomes for youth is especially important in South Africa, where youth represent a very large part of the working age population. While across OECD countries youth (15-29) only represent 20% of the total population and 30% of the working age population (15-64), these shares amount to 29% and 44% in South Africa (Figure 1.5). The large share of youth in the labour market reflects one of South Africa's key advantages: a large and growing working age population. This demographic shift gives South Africa substantial growth potential, provided the growing working age population can be employed productively. However, as the unemployment and inactivity numbers show, South Africa has so far not been able to take full advantage of this demographic dividend. To fully capitalise on its demographic opportunities, South Africa has to invest in job creation and human capital development (World Bank, 2015).

Labour market outcomes do not only differ strongly between age groups, but also by region. The unemployment rate (for the population aged 15-64) in the fourth quarter of 2016 ranged from 19.3% in Limpopo to 34.7% in Free State. The differences in terms of discouraged workers are even more significant, with their share being limited to 1.5% in Western Cape but reaching a 21.1% in KwaZulu Natal. Based on the expanded definition of unemployment, which takes discouraged workers into account, the unemployment rate is lowest in Western Cape (23.6%) and highest in Nortern Cape (43.3%).

Figure 1.5. Population age structure, South Africa and OECD, 2015

Percentage of total population

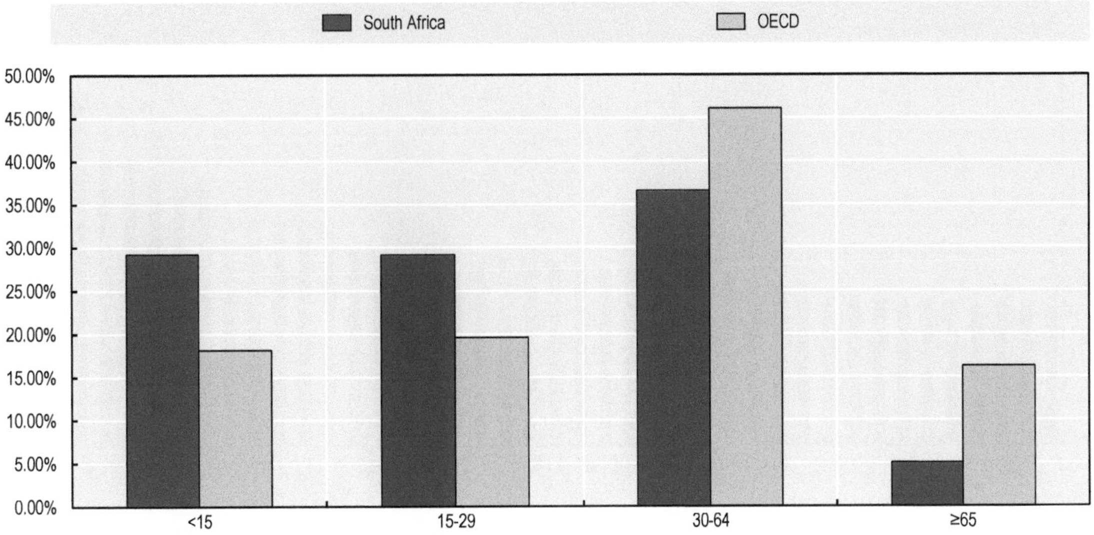

Source: World Bank, World Population Prospects: The 2015 Revision.

The state of the South African labour market reflects the Apartheid legacy, with significant differences in outcomes between population groups.[1] The unemployment rate (for the population aged 15-64) of the Black African population (30.0% in the fourth quarter of 2016) and Coloured population (22.0%) largely exceeds that of Indians/Asians (11.1%) and Whites (6.6%). The contrast is even bigger when using the expanded definition of unemployment (40.1% of Black Africans, 9.1% of Whites). An equally big difference exists in labour force participation rates between Black Africans (57.8%) and Whites (67.4%).

These large labour market inequalities are reflected in the overall level of income inequality in the country. With a Gini coefficient of 63.4 (with 0 representing perfect equality and 100 perfect inequality) in 2011, South Africa is one of the most unequal of countries worldwide for which data are available data (World Bank World Development Indicators). Inequality is much higher than among OECD countries, where the Gini ranges from around 25 (Slovenia, the Slovak Republic, Norway, the Czech Republic) to around 50 (Chile and Mexico) (Figure 1.6). Countries like Brazil and Colombia had similarly high inequality levels at the start of the century, but while inequality increased in South Africa, these countries were able to reduce inequality.

Migration movements represent important inflows and outflows of skills. The proportion of international migrants in the South African population has been growing steadily during the last 15 years. In 2015, 5.8% of the South African population was foreign born, compared to only 2.2% in 2000 (United Nations, 2016). Compared with other upper middle income countries, where international migrants account on average for 1.4% of the population, South Africa has a large immigrant population. About three quarters of migrants in South Africa originate from other African countries, with the largest number of migrants coming from Mozambique, Zimbabwe and Lesotho (2013 data, United Nations).

Figure 1.6. Income inequality, OECD and partner countries, 2000-12

Gini index (0-100)

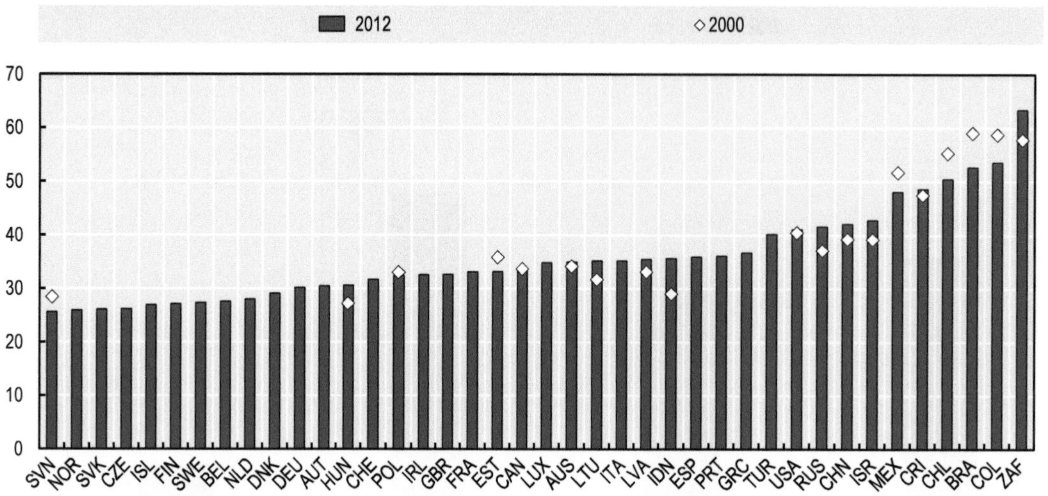

Note: 2013 for Chile and United States, 2011 for South Africa and Germany, 2010 for Canada, Australia, Indonesia, China and Israel. 2001 for Israel and Australia, 1999 for Brazil, China and Indonesia, 1998 for Latvia and Slovenia.

Source: World Bank, World Development Indicators.

While South Africa is a relatively popular destination country for immigrants, especially compared with other sub-Saharan African countries, many people also leave the country to settle abroad. In 2010, 1.6% of the people born in South Africa were living in OECD countries. Among high-skilled South Africans, this share reaches 12.2%. High-skilled emigration has been growing fast, with the share increasing by 5.3 percentage points in the period 2000-10. Moreover, South Africa is among the top 30 countries with the highest absolute number of tertiary educated emigrants (World Bank Group, 2016). The main OECD destinations for South African emigrants are the United Kingdom, Australia, the United States, New Zealand and Canada. The labour market outcomes of South Africans living in OECD countries are very good, with an unemployment rate of only 6% (4.1% among the highly educated) and a 76.5% employment rate (84.6% among the highly educated). Emigration remains very popular among South Africans, as 15% of South Africans say they would move permanently if they had the opportunity. The emigration option is most popular among youth (23%) and high-skilled (18%) (OECD, 2015).

Contrary to most OECD countries, the foreign born population in South Africa has better labour market outcomes than the native born population (Fauvelle-Aymar, 2014). The unemployment rate of international migrants (14.7%) is lower than that of non-migrants (26.1%) and domestic migrants (32.5%). International migrants are also less likely to be discouraged, as only 3.8% is considered to be a discouraged jobseeker, compared to 8.4% of non-migrants and 6.8% of domestic migrants. Evidence suggests that the higher probability of employment of international migrants in South Africa is irrespective of differences in age, gender, level of education, ethnical background and region of residence (Fauvelle-Aymar, 2014). Hence, while international migrants are more likely to have completed tertiary education, this cannot explain the difference in unemployment rates.

While the relatively low unemployment rate of international migrants suggests that these individuals have positive labour market outcomes in South Africa, the picture looks different when focussing on their job quality. International migrants are much more likely to be employed in the informal sector (32.7% compared to 16.6% for non-migrants), and over half of employed international migrants are in precarious employment (53.29% compared to 30.3% of non-migrants). Evidence suggests that the higher probability of international migrants to be employed in the informal sector or in precarious jobs is not linked to differences in age, gender, level of education, ethnical background or region of residence (Fauvelle-Aymar, 2014). Doyle et al. (2014) also find evidence for substantial 'brain waste', as skilled immigrants in South Africa often work in low-skilled jobs. The probability of getting a skilled job differs between the countries of origin, with educated non-South Africans having the highest chance of ending up in low-skilled (informal) jobs.

Around 17% of employment in South Africa in 2015 was in the informal sector.[2] The probability of being employed in the informal sector is highest for black Africans and low-skilled (incomplete high school or below) workers (Statistics South Africa, 2015a). The share of the informal sector is largest in the trade, construction and transport sectors, while it is negligible in the mining industry. In South Africa, however, many people work in precarious jobs even outside the informal sector. This is reflected in the share of employment in the "informal economy", which includes all persons working in the informal sector as well as those persons working in the formal sector who are not entitled to basic benefits or protection. The ILO (2012) estimates the informal economy in South Africa to represent around 33% of total employment. The relative size of the South African informal economy is comparable to China (32.6%), and is smaller than in most other upper-middle income countries (with the exception of European countries).

Key education and skills trends and facts

Educational attainment in South Africa is on the rise, but remains low compared with OECD countries. In 2015, 35% of the South Africans aged 25-64 had below upper secondary educational attainment, 56% had upper secondary and post-secondary non-tertiary educational attainment, and only 8% had tertiary educational attainment (UNESCO Education Database). In comparison to many other upper-middle income countries, South Africa has a large share of the population with at least upper-secondary education, but a relatively small share of tertiary educated individuals. While there has been a substantial shift from lower secondary education to upper secondary, the share of individuals with tertiary education has only increased modestly (from around 5% in the early 2000s). Nonetheless, this modest increase in tertiary attainment shares represents a doubling of the number of South Africans with tertiary education. The share of individuals without any education dropped spectacularly from 12.3% in 2002 to 5.9% in 2015. The improvement in educational attainment in South Africa is also clear when focussing on the group of 25-34 year-olds, as almost three quarters of them have upper secondary or post-secondary non-tertiary educational attainment (*OECD Education Database*).

While there was a substantial gap between educational attainment of men and women in the mid-1990s, especially for secondary and tertiary education, the difference had almost completely disappeared by 2010 (Statistics South Africa, 2015b). The gap in educational attainment between different population groups has also decreased over time, but substantial differences remain. While only 0.8% of the white population in 2011 had no schooling, this share amounted to 8.2% among the black African population. Moreover, the gap between the proportion of whites and black Africans completing secondary education is about the same size in 2010 as it was in 1950, while the gap for tertiary education actually increased. The difference in average education level between native South Africans and international migrants is small, but this average hides a strong difference in the distribution of education. Compared to native South Africans, the educational profile of migrants is more polarised, with a larger share being tertiary educated (6.5 percentage point difference) and a larger share having no schooling (2.7 percentage point difference) (Fauvelle-Aymar, 2014).

The performance of South Africa in international skills assessments, such as TIMSS, gives an indication of the quality of the South African education system. In the last round of the TIMSS survey, which measures mathematics and science skills of eighth grade students (around 14 years old)[3] across a range of countries, South Africa ranked 38th out of 39 participating countries in mathematics and last in science (Mullis et al., 2016). Figure 1.7 shows that South Africa's average test score is low compared to participating OECD and upper-middle income countries.[4] Although South African students' skill level remained low in the 2015 evaluation, it had increased substantially compared to 2002 and 2011 (Department of Basic Education, 2013). Between 2002 and 2011 the greatest improvement was among the 'most disadvantaged' learners, who scored the lowest initially (Reddy et al., 2012). However, big differences remained between students from different types of schools (public versus independent) and schools with different historical background.

Figure 1.7. Mathematics performance of eight graders, South Africa and OECD, and upper-middle income participating countries, 2015

Average mathematics and science score (TIMSS)

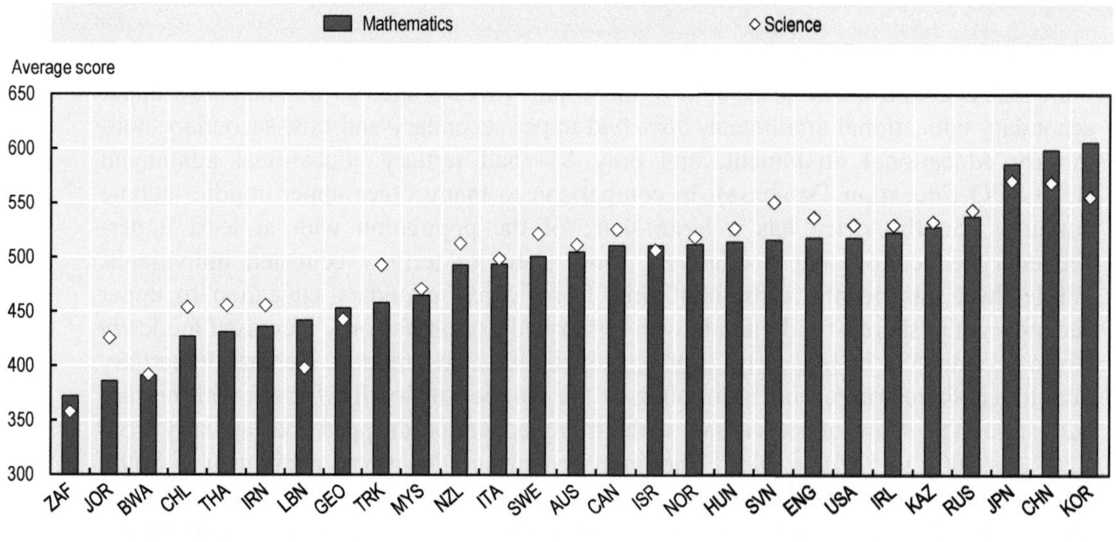

Note: China only includes Taipei.

Source: Mullis et al. (2016).

In 2014, over 2 million students and learners were enrolled in South African post-school education and training.[5] The number of participants has been rising steadily over the last years. The majority of these students (51%) were enrolled in higher education institutions, 36% in technical and vocational education and training colleges and 13% in adult education and training centres. Participation in technical and vocational training has been on the rise, as its share in total post-school education and training increased by 12 percentage points during the period 2010-14.

Public spending on education, expressed relative to GDP, is high in South Africa, reaching 6% in 2013 (*OECD WISE Database*). Only a few OECD countries have higher relative public spending on education, namely Belgium, Denmark, Finland, Iceland, New Zealand, Norway and Sweden (2011 data). However, spending on education is spread over a larger number of individuals in South Africa, given its relatively young population compared to the OECD average (Figure 1.5), and therefore spending per student can be a more useful indicator. Government expenditure per student in primary and secondary education in South Africa, expressed relative to GDP per capita, is below the OECD average (UNESCO Database). Expenditure per student at the tertiary level (relative to GDP per capita), on the other hand, is higher than in most OECD countries. In comparison to OECD countries, capital expenditure represents a smaller share of total expenditure by public education institutions in South Africa and a significantly larger share of current expenditure is devoted to teacher compensation.

Skills shortage and mismatch

The existence of shortages of skilled workers is often cited as a main factor contributing to limited growth prospects for South Africa. In its National Development Plan, South Africa identifies its poor skills profile as a key reason for being in a "low growth, middle income trap". The third National Skills Development Strategy also identifies continuing shortages in the artisanal, technical and professional field as one of the pressing challenges that have an impact on the ability of South Africa's economy to expand and to provide more employment opportunities. One of the commitments made in this skills development strategy is therefore to "increase the number of appropriately skilled people to meet the demands of our current and emerging economic and social development".

According to the results of the 2015 Manpower Global Talent Shortage Survey (ManpowerGroup, 2015), 31% of South African employers report having difficulties filling jobs. While this share is below the global average (38%), it rose drastically compared to the year before (when only 8% reported difficulties). The biggest difficulties are reported for jobs in skilled trades, engineering, and management. The existence of skill shortages in South Africa is reflected in its place in the IMD World Talent Ranking, which measures the extent to which countries develop, attract and retain talent (IMD World Competitiveness Center, 2015). South Africa holds the 51st place out of 61 countries in the ranking. The ranking is based on three components: i) investment and development, ii) appeal, and iii) readiness. Whereas South Africa has an average performance on the second component (34th out of 61), it is among the bottom performers for the first (55) and third (54) component. South Africa ranks among the bottom five countries for worker motivation, the availability of skilled labour, the implementation of apprenticeships, the pupil-teacher ratio in basic education, the ability of the educational system to meet the needs of a competitive economy, and the emphasis on science in schools. These indicators, with the exception of the pupil-teacher ratio, are based on replies from executives in top- and middle managements to an executive opinion survey.

Shortages often go hand in hand with the existence of qualification mismatch, when employers hire workers who do not have the right qualification for the job. Comparable international evidence on qualification mismatch dates back to 2005 (OECD, 2011), and showed that the incidence of overqualification in South Africa (24.2%) was just below the OECD average (25.3%), while underqualification was more widespread in South Africa (27.6%) than on average across OECD countries (22.4%).[6] Other included upper-middle income countries (Brazil, Mexico and Turkey), have a much lower incidence of underqualification (unweighted average of 7.9%) and a much higher incidence of overqualification (37.6%) than South Africa. These numbers are consistent with the existing shortages of skilled workers.

New evidence on the existence of skills shortages and mismatch has recently been developed by the OECD in its *Adapting to Changing Skill Needs* report (OECD, 2017a). The indicators are available for European countries and South Africa, and have been made comparable across this set of countries. Mismatch is measured both in terms of qualifications and field-of-study. The evidence shows that in 2015, 52.3% of South African workers were employed in an occupation for which they did not have the correct qualification. About 27.9% of individuals work in occupations for which a higher level of qualification would be required, i.e. they are underqualified for their occupation. A further 24.4% is employed in occupations that normally require a lower level of qualification (overqualification). The incidence of qualification mismatch in South Africa is higher than in European countries, where only 33.6% of workers in 2015 were mismatched in terms of qualification level. Moreover, none of the European countries has a higher incidence of qualification mismatch than South Africa. Mismatch in terms of field-of-study is also higher in South Africa (32.6%) than in Europe (31.5%), but the difference is smaller. As field-of-study is only available for individuals with vocational or post-secondary degrees, the data refer to a relatively small part of the South African population (Figure 1.8).

In addition to information on qualification and field-of-study mismatch, the new OECD Skills for Jobs database (OECD, 2017a) provides detailed information on the occupations and skills in shortage or surplus in European countries and South Africa. These Skill Needs indicators are constructed using information on employment, unemployment, hours worked, hourly wages and underqualification. Figure 1.9 provides an overview of the degree of shortage or surplus of different skills in South Africa. Positive values signal shortages, whereas negative values signal surpluses. Surpluses are mainly found in skills related to manual tasks, like physical strength, manufacturing and production knowledge and technical skills. Shortages, on the other hand arise mainly in cognitive skills, such as complex problem solving skills and quantitative abilities, as well as in higher skilled knowledge fields like education and health care. This pattern clearly reflects the oversupply of low-skilled workers and undersupply of high skilled workers in South Africa.

Figure 1.8. Qualification and field-of-study mismatch, Europe and South Africa, 2015

Share of employed, 15-64 (%)

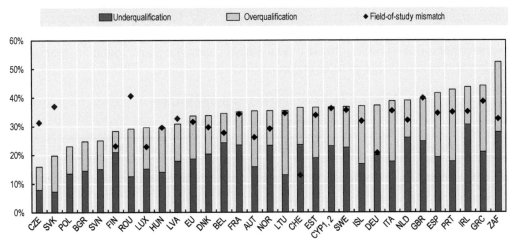

Note: Field-of-study mismatch not available for Poland, Bulgaria and Slovenia. EU is the unweighted average of the included European countries. Three-digit occupations with less than ten observations are excluded for the calculation of qualification mismatch. German data refer to 2013.

1. Note by Turkey: The information in this document with reference to "Cyprus" relates to the southern part of the Island. There is no single authority representing both Turkish and Greek Cypriot people on the Island. Turkey recognises the Turkish Republic of Northern Cyprus (TRNC). Until a lasting and equitable solution is found within the context of the United Nations, Turkey shall preserve its position concerning the "Cyprus issue".

2. Note by all the European Union Member States of the OECD and the European Union: The Republic of Cyprus is recognised by all members of the United Nations with the exception of Turkey. The information in this document relates to the area under the effective control of the Government of the Republic of Cyprus.

Source: *OECD Skills for Jobs Database.*

Figure 1.9. Skills shortage and surplus, South Africa, 2014

Knowledge, abilities and skills

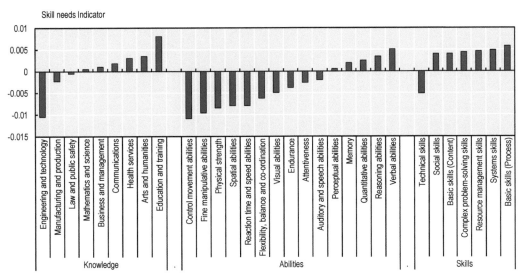

1. Positive values signal shortage, negative values signal surplus.

Source: *OECD Skills for Jobs Database.*

26 – 1. KEY DRIVERS OF SKILLS DEMAND AND SUPPLY IN SOUTH AFRICA

Going beyond the aggregate skill groups presented in Figure 1.9, Table 1.1 lists the top shortage and surplus skills observed in South Africa. The biggest shortages are observed in expression, comprehension and reasoning, as well as in skills related to business management, health and teaching (Table 1.1). The business management skills shortage is consistent with the documented need for more and better entrepreneurial skills (OECD, 2017b). The biggest surpluses are found in manual skills, but also in knowledge of sales and marketing.

Table 1.1. Skills most in shortage and surplus

Top 5 of knowledge, abilities and skills

Knowledge	Abilities	Skills
Top 5 shortage		
Economics and accounting	Written expression	Learning strategies
Administration and management	Written comprehension	Instructing
Education and training	Deductive reasoning	Management of personnel resources
Psychology	Inductive reasoning	Reading comprehension
Sociology and anthropology	Oral expression	Monitoring
Top 5 surplus		
Building and construction	Static strength	Operation and control
Mechanical	Multilimb co-ordination	Repairing
Design	Control precision	Equipment maintenance
Transportation	Reaction time	Troubleshooting
Sales and marketing	Manual dexterity	Operation monitoring

Source: OECD Skills for Jobs Database.

Notes

1. In South Africa, people self-identify into four population groups: Black African, Coloured, White or Indian/Asian. The Coloured group refers to individuals with mixed ethnic backgrounds. In 2015, the Black African population group accounted for 80.5% of the entire population, the Coloured group for 8.8%, the White group for 8.3%, and the Indian/Asian group for the remaining 2.5% (Statistics South Africa, 2015c).

2. The informal sector in South Africa is defined as i) employees working in establishments that employ fewer than five employees, who do not deduct income tax from their salaries/wages, and ii) employers, own-account workers and persons helping unpaid in their household business who are not registered for either income tax or value-added tax.

3. In South Africa, grade 9 students rather than grade 8 students participate to TIMSS. Their average age is 16.

4. In 2015 South Africa participated for the first time in the Grade 4 TIMSS assessment (for mathematics only). The results are similar to the 8-grade results, with South Africa ranking 48th among 49 participating countries.

5. Post-school education included all learning activities in the higher education and training phase (provided by higher education institutes), all learning activities in TVET colleges (i.e. non-academic learning above grade 9) and all adult learning and training activities.

6. The mismatch data for South Africa from OECD (2011) and the new evidence presented in this report are not fully consistent because they are based on different datasets and on a slightly modified methodology.

References

Department of Basic Education (2013), *Macro Indicator Report*, Republic of South Africa.

Doyle, A., A.C. Peters and A. Sundaram (2014), "Skills Mismatch and Informal Sector Participation Among Educated Immigrants: Evidence from South Africa", *SALDRU Working Paper*, No. 137.

Fauvelle-Aymar, C. (2014), "Migration and Employment in South Africa: An Econometric Analysis of Domestic and International Migrants (QLFS (Q3) 2012)", *MiWORC Report*, No. 6.

Fedderke, J.W., and F. Pirouz (2002), "The Role of Mining in the South African Economy", *South African Journal of Economic and Management Sciences*, Vol. 5, No. 1, pp. 1-34.

IMD World Competitiveness Center (2015), *IMD World Talent Report 2015*, Institute for Management Development, Lausanne.

ManpowerGroup (2015), *Talent Shortage Survey 2015*, ManpowerGroup.

Mullis, I.V.S.et al. (2016), *TIMSS 2015 International Results in Mathematics*, Retrieved from Boston College, TIMSS & PIRLS International Study Center website.

OECD (2017a), *Getting Skills right: Skills for Jobs Indicators*, OECD Publishing, Paris, http://dx.doi.org/10.1787/9789264277878-en.

OECD (2017b), *OECD Economic Survey – South Africa*, OECD Publishing, Paris.

OECD (2016), *OECD Employment Outlook 2016*, OECD Publishing, Paris, http://dx.doi.org/10.1787/empl_outlook-2016-en.

OECD (2015), *Connecting with Emigrants: A Global Profile of Diasporas 2015*, OECD Publishing, Paris, http://dx.doi.org/10.1787/9789264239845-en.

OECD (2014), *OECD Science, Technology and Industry Outlook 2014*, OECD Publishing, Paris, http://dx.doi.org/10.1787/sti_outlook-2014-en.

OECD (2011), *OECD Employment Outlook 2011*, OECD Publishing, Paris, http://dx.doi.org/10.1787/empl_outlook-2011-en.

Reddy, V. et al. (2012), *Highlights from TIMSS 2011: The South African Perspective*, HSRC, Pretoria.

Statistics South Africa (2016), *Labour Market Dynamics in South Africa, 2015*, Statistics South Africa, Pretoria.

Statistics South Africa (2015a), *Labour Market Dynamics in South Africa, 2014*, Statistics South Africa, Pretoria.

Statistics South Africa (2015b), *Census 2011: A Profile of Education Enrolment, Attainment and Progression in South Africa*, Statistics South Africa, Pretoria.

Statistics South Africa (2015c), *Mid-year Population Estimates 2015*, Statistics South Africa, Pretoria.

United Nations (2016), *International Migration Report 2015*, United Nations, New York.

World Bank (2015), "South Africa Economic Update: Jobs and South Africa's Changing Demographics", *South Africa Economic Update*; No. 7, World Bank Group, Washington, D.C.

World Bank Group (2016), *Migration and Remittances Factbook 2016, Third Edition*, World Bank, Washington, DC.

World Economic Forum (2016), *The Global Competitiveness Report 2016-2017*, World Economic Forum, Geneva.

Database references

OECD Education Database, http://www.oecd.org/education/database.htm.

OECD Employment Database, http://www.oecd.org/employment/emp/onlineoecdemploymentdatabase.htm.

OECD National Accounts Database, http://www.oecd-ilibrary.org/fr/economics/data/oecd-national-accounts-statistics_na-data-en.

OECD Skills for Jobs Database, https://stats.oecd.org.

OECD WISE Database, http://www.oecd.org/employment/skills-for-employment-indicators.htm.

Chapter 2

Skills assessment and anticipation system in South Africa

In order to design policies that effectively tackle existing or anticipated skills imbalances, countries must thoroughly analyse their demand for and supply of skills. The findings from these skills needs assessment exercises can feed into a range of policies, such education and training, employment and migration policies, to make them more responsive to labour market needs. This chapter documents the different skill needs assessment exercises put in place in South Africa, highlighting the various information sources and stakeholders involves.

For skills to be developed and utilised in the most efficient way, countries must understand the supply and demand of skills. As such, it is important that countries develop relevant skills assessment and anticipation exercises. Countries differ widely in term of methods used to identify their skill needs, but also in terms of the level at which these exercises are conducted and the stakeholder involvement (OECD, 2016). South Africa has put in place multiple exercises to measure their skill needs, and a range of stakeholders have been involved.

Since 2014 the Department for Higher Education and Training (DHET) has produced two lists of occupations most in demand. While the methodology for defining this list has changed over time, it generally relies on information from a large range of sources. For the compilation of the list, DHET uses a combination of data analysis, econometric modelling, literature reviews and stakeholder engagement.

In terms of data analysis, DHET looks at employment growth by occupation from the Quarterly Labour Force Survey. Additionally, vacancy statistics produced by the Department of Labour are analysed. The Department of Labour produces an annual report on unemployment and vacancies, "Job Opportunities and Unemployment in the South African Labour Market". This report takes stock of unemployment and vacancy evolutions in South Africa and its provinces. Vacancy data, based on information collected from newspapers, is provided through the Job Opportunity Index database and is available at the occupational and industry level. The data presented in these reports have been used to make assessments of the existing shortages. The 2014 report, for example, concludes that there are "continuing skills shortages in the artisanal, technical and professional fields that are fundamental to the development and growth of our economy".

In addition to current labour market information, DHET takes output from a macro-education forecasting tool into account to predict which occupations will grow strongest over the next year. This tool provides employment prospects for a set of 45 occupations and sectors, and allows assessing future imbalances by educational qualifications.[1] The forecasting tool combines a macro-economic model of South Africa with models of supply and demand for occupations and educational qualifications. The model starts from macro-economic projections of future labour demand for the entire economy and for sectors. By feeding in information on the link between demand for labour, occupations and educational attainment, on replacement demand for occupations, and on the supply of educational qualifications, the model aims to forecast demand for about 400 detailed occupations and predict future imbalances.

Also included in the list of occupations in high demand are the occupations that are mentioned in strategic documents, such as the National Development Plan, the New Growth Path, the Industrial Policy Action Plan and the Joint Initiative on Priority Skills Acquisition (JIPSA). Influential research papers, such as the HRDC report on the production of professionals and the Career Junction salary and wage report, are also consulted to determine occupations in demand. Finally, the list relies on the analysis of scarce skills from the Sector Employment and Training Authorities (SETAs) and from the Strategic Integrated Projects (SIPs).

The SETAs, established in the 1998 Skills Development Act, have the mandate of developing sector skills plans, promoting learnerships,[2] and distributing the skills development levy paid by employers. As part of their Sector Skills plan, SETAs identify which skills or occupations are in shortage in their sector. For this the SETAs use information from employers, mainly from their Workplace Skills Plans (WSP) and Annual Training Report (ATR). Employers are required to develop a WSP that assesses the type and amount of training needed in the coming year based on current and future skill needs. Methods for assessing which occupations to include in the scarce skill list of their Sector Skill Plans differ widely across SETAs. The Manufacturing Engineering and Related Services SETA (MERSETA), for example, uses fixed thresholds on the share and number of employers reporting scarcity for the occupation and on the absolute and relative number of vacancies. These quantitative rules are only applied to occupations with a sufficient number of employees. Qualitative assessments of the absolute and relative number of vacancies are used in small occupations. A draft list is reviewed by members from the industry and their comments are included. In the Chemical Industries SETA (CHIETA) the scarce skill list is entirely based on the answers of employers to the questions in their Workplace skills plan (whether they experienced scarcity in a specific occupation and the number of hard-to-fill vacancies because of scarcity in that occupation), and on workshops with stakeholders. The Fibre Processing and Manufacturing SETA uses forecasts of growth demand and replacement demand to determine which occupations are scarce. Rasool (2015) argues that there is an urgent need for SETAs to capture occupational demand information in a more accurate, valid and reliable way.

In 2012 South Africa adopted a National Infrastructure Plan, which set out big projects of infrastructure creation and upgrading. The goal of these projects is to transform the economic landscape, while creating jobs and strengthening the delivery of basic services. The plan contains 18 SIPs covering social and economic infrastructure in all provinces. To ensure that the necessary skills are available in the workforce for these projects, a common methodology was developed to compile a list of occupations in demand at the national, provincial and sectoral level. The methodology consists of 21 steps that can be followed from the demand to the supply side. Tools, such as templates and prototypes have been developed to facilitate the 21 step process. The process involves input from a variety of sources, ranging from the macro-education forecasting model, to expertise from training providers and employers. The procedure goes beyond identifying which skills are in shortage (and the corresponding size, timing and location of these shortages), but also provides guidelines on how to solve the identified scarcities. Details for the 21 steps are provided in Box 2.1. The development of these SIPs skills plans generally involves a broad set of related stakeholders, such as employers, training providers and professional bodies.

Box 2.1. Strategic Integrated Projects: 21 steps

What skills are needed?

1. Develop a list of SIP projects (clustered into sectors).
2. Develop skills prototypes consisting of the occupations needed for a typical project with an initial estimation of the scarcity of each occupation, derived from the experience of project managers.
3. Estimate total skills required for all projects.
4. Determine the national demand for occupations identified as scarce in STEP 3 (based on macro-model).
5. Set up Occupational Teams (OTs) to act as expert advisers per occupation. An OT is composed of theory and practical training providers, employers and those from registering or certifying bodies. Their initial role is to gather data and input from their communities of expert practice to refine the demand model.
6. Determine the number of people with the required occupational skills both in the workforce and who are unemployed (Labour Force Survey and Public Employment Service)
7. Estimate the number of those entering the labour market with the required skills.
8. Determine which occupations are not being developed at the required rate to meet the demand.
9. Provide an indication of the scale, place and timeframe of demand for each occupation.

What should be done?

10. Encourage those issuing tenders to include the relevant Training Standard (Construction Industry Development Board)
11. Consider schools in the area as feeders for training. Provide career guidance and support for gateway subjects such as in mathematics and science.
12. Determine which education and training providers should focus on developing which skills
13. The OT for each priority occupation should visit Centres of Specialisation and determine their capacity and support required.
14. Find workplace-based learning opportunities for needed occupations
15. Secure resources for the OT plan from SETAs, NSF and other sources.
16. Monitor and evaluate implementation. Funded plans must be implemented. In addition, simple, streamlined systems for monitoring and evaluation must be put in place

The special case of government

17. Determine which municipal, provincial or national departments need to play a role
18. Define the roles each must play and determine their skill requirements, match these against available skills and determine priorities/gaps.
19. Put together a plan and identify resources.
20. Implement, monitor and evaluate these plans for government capacity building.

Governance

21. Establish a robust governance structure to oversee the implementation of project implementation plans

Source: SIP skills portal (https://sip-skills.onlinecf.net/).

Using these different sources of information, DHET develops a draft list of occupations in high demand. To determine whether an occupation is included in the list, a scoring method is used, depending on how often an occupation is found to be in high demand. Allocated scores also vary by source of information (e.g. 5 points for occupations from the National Development Plan, 10 points for occupations from JIPSA). Occupations that require at least three years of formal education are rewarded additional points. After compilation, the draft list is reviewed by a range of stakeholders through a "Call for Evidence". These stakeholders include professional and statutory bodies, employers and employee bodies, educational institutions, other government departments, DHET entities, academic institutions and state-owned enterprises (parastatals). This consultation can result in the addition or removal of some occupations to/from the list.

As the process of skill needs assessment in South Africa is still in its early stages, the government has been consulting with the research community to optimise data collection and analysis. In 2002 the DHET launched the Labour Market Intelligence Partnership (LMIP), which is a research consortium consisting of researchers from the Development Policy Research Unit at the University of Cape Town and from the Centre for Researching Education and Labour at the University of Witwatersrand. The goal of the LMIP is to provide advice on the set up of a credible institutional mechanism for skills planning, as such contributing to evidence-based skills development. To that end, the LMIP has already set out a skills planning information framework and identified associated key indicators. The project relies on existing data sources from government departments, SETAs and education institutions. Additionally, the LMIP endeavours to build new data sources. One of the key outputs of the LMIP is the 2016 report on skills supply and demand in South Africa (Reddy et al., 2016), which provides a thorough picture of the supply and demand for skills, and the associated imbalances.

In order to better measure skill needs in South Africa, the LMIP has proposed a set of key indicators that capture different aspects related to skills demand and supply. The indicators cover six areas: i) economic context, ii) stock and flow of skills (supply), iii) demand, iv) replacement demand, v) future demand, and vi) education and training outcomes. The different indicators that are used to assess each broad area are described in Box 2.2. While most of the information for the assessment can be retrieved from currently available data sources, the LMIP has been researching the development of a new survey to be able to better measure the supply of training and skills demand. This SETA Labour Market Survey should collect detailed training and labour market information from employers through the SETAs. This information should be directly relevant to the labour market in which the SETAs operate. The new survey was already piloted in the Manufacturing, Engineering and Related Services SETA (MERSETA). The availability of information on education and training outcomes is currently very limited, and new surveys have to be developed to measure these indicators. Whereas some tracer studies have been implemented to assess education and training outcomes, these have generally been limited in scope. The LMIP has been experimenting with new tracer studies across different sectors (university, TVET college, community college and workplace learning), making substantial progress in standardising research methodologies and identifying how these studies could be institutionalised (Rogan, 2016; LMIP, 2015).

Box 2.2. LMIP key indicators for skill needs assessment

The Labour Market Intelligence Partnership (LMIP) has developed a framework for skill needs assessment. Related to this framework, a set of key indicators were identified in six broad areas.

1. Economic context

    1. Economic drivers (GDP, exports, investments)
    2. Demographic changes

2. Supply: Stock and flow of skills

    1. Grade 9 and 12 pass rates
    2. Enrolment and graduation rates at higher education and TVET colleges
    3. Immigration rates
    4. Training in the workplace*

3. Demand

    1. Sectors and occupations of employment
    2. Job vacancies
    3. Skills gaps (critical skills)*
    4. Earnings
    5. Hard-to-fill vacancies
    6. gGobal demand

4. Replacement demand

    1. Turnover of personnel*
    2. Mortality rates
    3. Retirement form workforce*
    4. Emigration rates

5. Future demand

    1. Changes in population
    2. Projections in economic growth
    3. Skills signals for government growth priorities
    4. Skills signals for new and potential businesses

6. Education and training outcomes

    1. Pipeline form schooling
    2. NEET
    3. Access to and outcomes of universities and TVET colleges
    4. Access to and outcomes of artisanal programmes
    5. Access to and outcomes of community programmes and adult education centres
    6. Workplace learning programme
    7. Instructors' education qualifications

The indicators with an asterisk will rely on data from the newly developed SETA Labour Market Survey. The availability of indicators for education and training outcomes, with the exception of NEET, will depend on the development of new datasets.

Source: LMIP (2015).

Notes

1. The forecasting tool was developed by the Wits Educational Policy Unit in partnership with Applied Development Research Solutions. The former, which is now known as the Centre for Researching Education and Labour (REAL), is a research centre at the University of Witwatersrand's School of Education, while the latter is an independent specialist organisation active in the fields of economic modelling, policy research and training services.

2. Learnerships were introduced in South Africa in the Skills Development Act of 1998 to replace the existing apprenticeship system. The main difference between the two systems is that apprenticeships were limited to trades, while learnerships can be implemented in a wide range of occupations. Further differences exist in terms of duration, contract type and evaluation methods. The learnership system never fully replaced the apprenticeship system, and apprentices still exist. Throughout this report the term learnership will be used to refer to both learnerships and apprenticeships.

References

LMIP –Labour Market Intelligence Partnership (2015), "Labour Market Intelligence Partnership Update 2015", South Africa.

OECD (2016), *Getting Skills Right: Assessing and Anticipating Changing Skill Needs*, OECD Publishing, Paris, http://dx.doi.org/10.1787/9789264252073-en.

Rasool, H. (2015), "Occupations in High Demand: Green Skills Methodology Case Study".

Reddy, V. et al. (2016), *Skills Supply and Demand in South Africa*, LMIP Publication, Human Sciences Research Council, Pretoria.

Rogan, M. (2016), "Tracing Graduates into the Labour Market", *HSRC Review*, Vol. 15, No. 3.

Chapter 3

Policies addressing skills imbalances in South Africa

As skills imbalances can be costly for individuals and societies, countries try to reduce them by implementing policies that steer the demand for and supply of skills. The demand for skills can, for example, be influenced by industrial policy, while education and training policies, as well as migration policies, can alter the supply of skills. This chapter looks at the policies that have been implemented in South Africa to tackle skills imbalances. The main focus of the chapter is on government policies, but interesting NGO and private sector initiatives are also highlighted.

Development strategies

Over the years, South Africa has formulated several development strategies and plans within which skills often play a key role. These strategies and plans set out the broad direction for South Africa in terms of skills development, and serve as guidelines for the development of more specific skills policies. These documents reflect the importance of skills for the overall development of the country.

In 2012, the South African Government launched the *National Development Plan*, which aims to eliminate poverty and reduce inequality by 2030. The plan provides a broad strategic framework to guide key choices and actions. While it is a plan for the whole economy, requiring progress on a broad front, three overall main priorities can be identified: i) raising employment through faster growth, ii) improving quality of education, skills development and innovation, and iii) building the capacity of the state to play a developmental, transformative role. Objectives in terms of employment include reducing the unemployment rate from 24.9% in 2012 to 6% in 2030 and raising the participation rate from 54% to 65%. Among the identified actions feature "position South Africa to attract offshoring services", "offer a tax incentive for employers hiring youth", "give a subsidy to the placement sector to identify, prepare and place matric students", and "adopt a more open immigration approach to expand supply of high-level skills". In terms of education and training, the Plan contains many objectives, among which increasing the share of learners who complete 12 years of schooling to 80 to 90%, providing 1 million learning opportunities through Community Education and Training Centres, producing 30 000 artisans per year, and increasing enrolment at universities by at least 70%. Actions to achieve these goals include strengthening and expanding the bursaries for teacher training, building a stronger relationship between the college sector and industry, and ensuring that all financially-needy students have access to appropriate funding.

In 2001, South Africa implemented its first *Human Resource Development Strategy* (HRDSA), which has its origins in the 1994 Reconstruction and Development Programme. The purpose of the HRDSA was to provide a plan to ensure that people are equipped to participate fully in society, to be able to find or create work, and to benefit fairly from it. The strategy put forward four strategic objectives: i) improving the foundations for human development, ii) improving the supply of high-quality skills which are more responsive to societal and economic need, iii) increasing employer participation in lifelong learning, and iv) supporting employment growth through industrial policies, innovation, research and development. In 2010 a new version of the HRDSA was launched, taking into account the shortcomings of the 2001 Strategy, such as the missing framework for monitoring and evaluation and the limited role for social partners, and new challenges. The new Strategy sets out fifteen strategic priorities for the period 2010-30, and defines a five-year medium term strategic framework identifying eight commitments. Each commitment has multiple strategic objectives, and indicators are defined to measure progress on the objectives. The focus of the five-year framework is on general education and training outcomes, increasing the supply of specific skills (e.g. engineers, artisans, R&D personnel), technology diffusion and access, and health outcomes.

A subcomponent of the HRDSA is the *National Skills Development Strategy* (NSDS), of which the first version was launched in 2001. The development of a NSDS was put forward in the 1998 Skills Development Act. The NSDS was updated in 2005, and once again in 2010. The current third version of the NSDS (NSDS III) focusses on eight goals: i) establishing a credible institutional mechanism for skills planning, ii) increasing access to occupationally-directed programmes, iii) promoting the growth of a public FET college system that is responsive to sector, local, regional and national skill needs and priorities, iv) addressing the low level of youth and adult language and numeracy skills to enable additional training, v) encouraging better use of workplace-based skills development, vi) encouraging and supporting co-operatives, small enterprises, worker-initiated, NGO and community training initiatives, vii) increasing public sector capacity for improved service delivery and supporting the building of a developmental state, and viii) building career and vocational guidance. For each goal outcomes and outputs have been identified, which are used for monitoring and evaluation. The key drivers of the NSDS III are the SETAs, DHET and the National Skills Fund.

In recent years, a growing consensus emerged in South Africa about the need for a new growth path if the country wants to create decent work, reduce inequality and defeat poverty. This new growth path should involve the restructuring of the South African economy to improve its performance in terms of labour absorption and the composition and rate of growth. To this end, the government is committed to identify areas where employment creation is possible on a large scale and develop a policy package to facilitate employment creation in these areas. The in 2010 released *New Growth Path* Framework targets to grow employment by 5 million jobs by 2020, drastically reducing the unemployment rate. To achieve this job creation target, the framework identifies five job drivers: i) direct employment creation through public infrastructure projects, ii) targeting of more labour-absorbing activities across all economic sectors, iii) taking advantage of new opportunities in the knowledge and green economies, iv) leveraging social capital in the social economy and the public services, and v) fostering rural development and regional integration. To achieve this, a developmental package consisting of macroeconomic strategies, microeconomic strategies and stakeholder commitment is developed.

To achieve the goals from the New Growth Path, strategies have been developed in different areas, such as skills, green economy and youth employment. The *National Skills Accord* has set out eight commitments to significantly increase the number of South Africans who can access training in order to increase the skills base of the economy. The accord is a partnership between organised labour, business representatives, the community constituency and government. The accord sets targets for workplace learning opportunities in the private and public sector (including state-owned enterprises) and employer spending on training, and commits to improving the SETA system and the FET colleges. Similarly, a *Basic Education and Partnerships with Schools Accord* was developed to address quality issues in basic education. The Accord focusses on the involvement of social partners in school development interventions, setting targets for the number of schools that will receive this kind of support.

Education and training: Policies targeting individuals

To guarantee a sufficient supply of skills, individuals might need additional incentives to invest in education and training. This is especially important in countries like South Africa, where educational attainment levels are relatively low. Financial incentives can increase access to education and training, especially for individuals from disadvantaged backgrounds. Special programmes for individuals without qualifications should lower the thresholds for them to participate in further training activities. Finally, providing good and easily accessible information on the availability of education and training options, and on the labour market outcomes of these options, should increase the supply of relevant skills.

Student loans and bursaries

Given the low levels of higher educational attainment in South Africa, it is important to provide individuals the opportunity to access higher education. The National Student Financial Scheme (NSFAS) was established in 1999, replacing its predecessor, the Tertiary Education Fund of South Africa (TEFSA, established in 1991). The NSFAS is responsible for providing loans and bursaries to financially needy and academically deserving students in public universities and TVET colleges. Until 2007, funding was limited to university students. The funds allocated through NSFAS (and its predecessor) have increased substantially over the years (Figure 3.1, Panel A), reaching ZAR 9 billion in 2014. Of these ZAR 9 billion, ZAR 7 billion was distributed to university students, and ZAR 2 billion to TVET college students. The funds assisted over 400 000 students, of which 45% were university students. About ZAR 4.8 billion was distributed to university and TVET students in the form of bursaries, and the remaining ZAR 4.2 billion went to convertible loans to university students. Unlike bursaries, loans have to be paid back to NSFAS after students have become employed earning above a minimum threshold. Up to 40% of the loan can, however, be converted in a non-repayable bursary based on academic performance. The main source of income for NSFAS was the Department for Higher Education and Training (DHET), providing 69% of the income for loans and bursaries (Figure 3.1, Panel B). Other substantial contributors to the NSFAS are the Department of Basic Education (11%) and the National Skills Fund (9%). Other government departments, universities, SETAs and the private sector also contribute to the scheme, albeit to a relatively small extent.

The large majority of bursaries provided by the NSFAS are general, i.e. not linked to specific university of TVET programmes. There are, however, a few large-size specialised bursary programmes that target education programmes that will lead to qualification that are in high demand. A first type of targeted bursary is the *Funza Lushaka Bursary Programme* from the Department of Basic Education, which focus on teaching qualifications in areas of national priority. Students receiving these bursaries are required to teach in public schools for the same number of years as they received the bursary. A second type of bursary is provided by the National Skills Funds (NSF), and targets university students with a study focus in a scarce skill area. No conditions are attached to this type of bursary. Non-DHET bursaries generally have a scarce skills focus, like the SETA bursaries that target the scarce skills identified in the Sector Skill Plans.

While the NSFAS funds have grown significantly over the last years, the main problem of the NSFAS is underfunding. A 2013 review report calculated that the NSFAS would need three times its budget to meet current demand (DHET, 2013). As a result of the underfunding, loans and bursaries are only granted to the very poor families with annual household incomes below ZAR 122 000. However, many families with incomes above this threshold cannot afford to fund their children's higher education. One factor contributing to the underfunding of the NSFAS is the low level of loan repayments. Estimates suggest that only about 20 to 25% of NSFAS loans are eventually repaid by the beneficiaries. The low repayment level can be linked to the very high dropout rate among NSFAS funded students, with only 28% of the recipients of NSFAS bursaries or loans (who are no longer studying) having completed their qualification.

Figure 3.1. NSFAS bursaries and loans

Panel A. Funding for bursaries and loans (in million ZAR, 1991-2014)

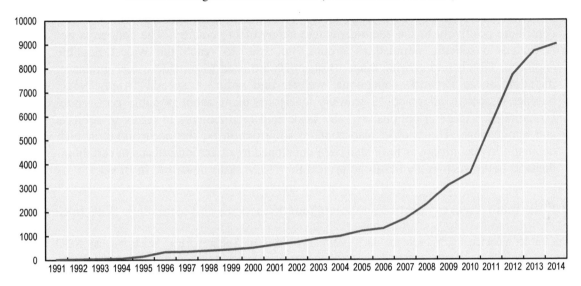

Panel B. Source of NSFAS funding (2014)

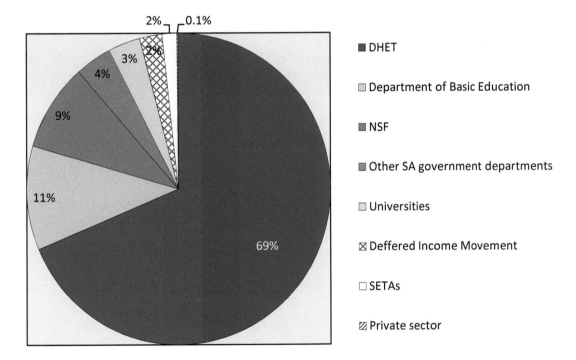

Source: NSFAS (2015).

Career guidance

An important step in ensuring that labour supply meets demand is the provision of career guidance, especially to students enrolled in secondary education and individuals seeking to re-skill or up-skill. The 2014 White Paper for Post-School Education and Training directed the DHET to establish Career Development Services. This Career Development Service was finally established in October 2014, and aims to have all South Africans citizens, irrespective of age of location, reach their full potential and contribute positively to the socio-economic status of the country. The service is not restricted to specific populations groups, but tries to reach the widest possible audience. To this end, a wide range of channels are used to provide career guidance, including social networks, telephone, website and radio. A special "Apply Now" booklet is sent to all grade 12 learners to inform them about possible post-school education and training options, and the associated requirements in terms of subjects and applications. The booklet also contains information on the occupations in high demand. Private initiatives have also been developed to attract individuals to certain in-demand fields, such as the Sci-Bono project for STEM skills described in Box 3.1.

Box 3.1. Sci-Bono discovery centre: Supporting maths, science and technology skills in Gauteng

In order to advance maths, science and technology skills in South Africa, Sci-Bono, an NGO mainly supported by the Gauteng Department of education, opened the Sci-Bono discovery centre in Johannesburg in 2004. Sci-bono takes a holistic approach to skills development, including projects to improver teaching quality, enhance learner performance, provide career advice, and promote and improve public awareness of science, engineering and technology.

Public awareness of science, engineering and technology

In its discovery centre, Sci-Bono organises a range of exhibitions and events that aim to make individuals, especially children and youth, more aware of and interested in science-related fields. Examples of events include a robotics tournament, monthly presentations by scientists, and the organisation of birthday parties. Sci-bono also participates in external science festivals and events.

School support programmes to enhance leaner performance

Sci-Bono manages projects to support schools in the Gauteng province to improve learner performance, mainly in maths, science and technical subjects. The flagship support programme, Secondary School Improvement Programme, offers additional tuition on Saturdays and during school holidays in priority schools. The programme also includes two-week intensive exam preparation camps. In 2014, 62 000 learners from 435 schools participated in the programme. Other projects include the Emasondosondo mobile science laboratory, the provision of audio-visual resources to support mathematics learning in grade 8 and 9, and the blended learning programme that offers free afternoon walk-in tuition to grade 12 learners.

Teacher training and development

Sci-Bono provides teacher training in mathematics, science, technology and technical subjects. Training focusses on content knowledge, assessment and lesson plan delivery. Downloadable lesson plans are made available on Sci-bono's website. During the period 2014-15 just over 3 200 teachers were trained, which is, as a result of insufficient funding, much lower than the target 21 650 teachers. However, the programme will be expanded extensively, as the Gauteng Department of Education has allocated a significant budget for the part of Sci-Bono's operations.

Box 3.1. Sci-Bono discovery centre: Supporting maths, science and technology skills in Gauteng
(cont.)

Career advice

Through its career education programmes and its counselling services, Sci-Bono assists learners to prepare for a life after school. A range of career education programmes have been implemented to provide information to learners, parents and out-of-school youth about education and employment opportunities in a wide range of sectors. Programmes include the Industry Focus Weeks, in which opportunities and innovation in critical sectors of the South African economy are highlighted and learners can interact with professionals, and "launch your career" workshops. Sci-Bono also employs qualified professionals who can give personal career advice for learners contacting Sci-Bono at the discovery centre's drop-in career information library or through the dedicated email address. Additionally, the centre offers testing and assessment services for learners and out-of-school clients.

An important source of career information provided by the Career Development Service is the National Career Advice Portal (NCAP) website, which gathers detailed information on a large range of occupations. For each occupation, the website provides details on the tasks, the required qualifications, the possible pathways to obtaining the required qualification (and the associated education providers), and on whether the occupation is in shortage or not (based on the DHET list of occupations in high demand). In the future, the website will be linked to information on available vacancies provided by the Department of Labour thought the Job Centres.

Second chance education

Given the high number of South Africans who did not complete lower secondary education (grade 9), the need for second chance education is considerable. While adult basic education featured among the policy priorities since the start of democracy in South Africa, it wasn't until the 2000 Adult Basic Education and Training (ABET) Act that the system was regulated. The act provided for the establishment, governance and funding of public adult learning centres, for the registration of private adult learning centres, and for quality assurance and quality promotion in adult basic education and training. The public adult learning centres focus on providing adults and youth with foundational skills. Private centres can sometimes have a broader scope, such as the Catholic Skills Centres supported by the Catholic Institute of Education which also provide workshop training (see Box 3.2). The ABET training is divided into four levels, equivalent to grades 0 to 9 in general education. Furthermore, ABET provides grades 10-12 training. When finishing level 4 a general education and training certificate for adults can be obtained. In 2014, the national senior certificate for adults was introduced, to give individuals who did not finish Matric the opportunity to obtain a qualification at the Matric level.[1] In 2014, about 260 000 learners were enrolled in public adult learning centres, and an additional 7 500 in private centres. Enrolment in public centres was highest in the ABET level 4 and grade 12 programmes, whereas in private centres it was highest in ABET level 1-3 programmes (DHET, 2014).

In addition, the 2014 White Paper on Post-school Education and Training, laid out the fundamentals for the establishment of a new type of adult learning institution: the Community Colleges. These Colleges are meant to build on the offering of the public Adult Learning Centres in order to expand vocational and skills-development programmes and non-formal programmes. The establishment and the role of the

Community Colleges was made more concrete in the 2015 National Policy on Community Colleges. Community Education and Training College Administrative centres have been set up in the nine provinces. The delivery sites of these Administrative Centers are referred to as Community Learning Centers. The former public adult learning centers have become such delivery sites. The Community Colleges are flexible in their programmes, with the offering being driven by community developmental priorities as well as priorities of the State. The Colleges provide for the development of both hard and soft skills. Aside from offering programmes that lead to formal qualifications, the Colleges can also offer, in collaboration with local authorities, SETAs, community organisations, other government departments and industry, non-formal programmes, which must take place on a needs basis.

Box 3.2. NGO skills development initiatives

Massive Open Online Varsity (MOOV)

The MOOV project tries to make high quality learning accessible to all, by providing access to high quality online courses from universities and platforms from all over the world. The project set up twelve MOOV centers in public libraries all over Johannesburg, mainly targeting the poorest areas (townships). Each center accommodates about 50 students at a time and is staffed by facilitators who are themselves graduates of MOOV. Everyone can participate in courses at the MOOV centers, without any fees or entry requirements. The focus of the offered courses is on computer science (e.g. web design) and business. After completing the course and successfully passing the assessment, students are awarded a certificate from the accrediting institution. The project is sponsored by the City of Johannesburg. The project has been growing rapidly, with 8 000 registered students and over 500 certificates obtained in the first 12 months after the project was launched.

Harambee Youth Employment Accelerator

At Harambee, employers looking for entry-level talent are connected to young, high-potential work-seekers who are locked out of the formal economy. The project focusses on youth with at least upper secondary education (Matric). Candidates with low levels of numeracy proficiency are provided with numeracy training through the Khan Academy. Furthermore, Harambee provides bridging courses aimed at improving the employability of the candidates. Harambee strives to match job seekers and employers as good as possible, by comparing the profile of candidates, created through psychometric and qualitative assessments, to the profile of employers. Since the launch of the project in 2011, Harambee has assessed nearly 300 000 youth, and placed 35 000 of them with some 300 South African businesses (Harambee, 2017). The Harambee project is co-financed by the South African Government, under the Jobs Fund.

Catholic Institute of Education

The Catholic Institute of Education (CIE) has set up a unit to support Skills Training Centres, where people who dropped out of the education system can develop skills that are needed in their communities. Different from the public adult learning centres, these Skills Centres do not only provide basic literacy and numeracy training, but non-formal training is also offered. In some areas community needs are assessed in co-operation with the Department of Social Development and through local discussion groups.

Source: Harambee (2017), "Breaking Barriers", *Quarterly Employment Report*, first quarter 2017.

Recognition of prior learning

Many South Africans do not have any formal degrees obtained in the education and training system. However, this does not necessarily imply that these individuals do not have any skills that are relevant for the labour market. Through work experience, people learn specific on-the-job skills. These skills are acquired informally or non-formally, and hence not accredited through a recognised qualification. People can, however, get these skills accredited through the process of Recognition of Prior Learning (RPL). The notion of RPL was introduced in South Africa at the start of democracy (1995), and has been particularly important to redress the inequalities created in the apartheid system. All qualifications from the National Qualification framework can be obtained in whole or in part through RPL. The system is mainly used for access to education, especially at the tertiary level, and to obtain credits for qualification (mainly at the general and further education level) (OECD, 2010). RPL remains a key policy area in South Africa, with a revision of the National Policy for the Implementation of the RPL launched in 2013 and a 2015 draft Policy on Artisan RPL. The new National Policy updates the 2002 version to align it to the last version of the National Qualification Framework. The artisan RPL policy sets out to have RPL as an active pathway to a full artisan trade occupational qualification in all sectors of the economy. It provides national criteria and guidelines on granting access to non-contracted learners to a national trade test.

While RPL can potentially be a strong policy tool in South Africa, the full potential does not seem to be reached so far. According to a 2008 OECD report (Gunning et al., 2008), take-up of RPL has been lower than expected. Evidence suggest that awareness of the existence of RPL is relatively low, and that even among the individuals who know about RPL's existence the understanding of its purpose is relatively limited (Makeketa and Maphalala, 2014). The assessment of prior learning activities often happens through a portfolio, which creates a barrier for the lower skilled who lack the literacy skills to put together these documents (Gunning et al., 2008). Furthermore, the collection of documents for the portfolio can be time-consuming, which is especially problematic for employed applicants (Marock, 2000). As there is no standard cost structure for RPL services, the costs can be borne by the applicants or the employers (or funded through sponsorships). These costs can be a substantial barrier, although according to SAQA RPL services and assessment cannot cost more than a full-time face-to-face programme.

National Skills Fund

In order to advance skills development in South Africa, the Skills Development Act established the National Skills Fund. The main purpose of the fund is to provide funding for national skills priorities, as defined in strategic documents as the NSDS and the HRDS. The fund is mainly used for investment in education and training of the South African population, for skills infrastructure development and for skills development research. The mandate of the skills fund is very broad, resulting in funding of a broad spectrum of projects. The strategic objectives of the NSF show a focus on skill development for disadvantaged groups, such as individuals in rural areas and SMMEs, and on the expansion and improvement of the post-school education and training system. Additionally, one of the objectives of the National Skills Fund is to develop skills for priority occupations, as such addressing skills imbalances. Examples of projects (co-)funded by the National Skills Fund are provided in Box 3.3.

In the financial year 2015/16 the NSF spent ZAR 4.697 billion on national skills development, benefiting almost 64 000 learners. Training of learners accounted for the largest part of investments (59%). Training was funded at universities (56%) and TVET colleges (16%), but also in the workplace (27%). While the majority of funding went to universities, funding of workplace based training reached the highest number of learners (47%, compared to 28% in universities). Aside from investment in training, the NSF also spent a substantial amount on strengthening the post-school education and training system (18% of spending), including the construction of three TVET college campuses and infrastructure projects in four universities. A further 21% of the total spending went to universities under the "no fees increase" agreement. This exceptional NFS spending was the result of the decision of the government not to increase university tuition fees for the 2016 academic year. Finally, 2% was spent on skills development research.

Box 3.3. National Skills Fund: Examples of funded projects

The Department of Rural Development and Land Reform established in 2010 the National Rural Youth Service Corps (NARYSEC), with the main goal to recruit and develop rural youth. The initiative provides a long-term training and employment programme for youth (aged 18 to 35) who completed grade 10, 11 or 12. Generally, six individuals per rural wards are recruited. Participants receive training to develop both their hard and soft skills. This training is targeted at the needs of the rural wards. After the intensive training period, the participants are employed in rural ward s to participate in social and economic development of rural areas. Participants who choose to become self-employed receive assistance and mentoring.

In 2012 the NSF concluded a five-year partnership with the Department of Correctional Services to provide access to occupationally-directed skills programmes in prison. The training is targeted towards skills that are needed in the labour market, as to increase the access to employment opportunities and entrepreneurship. The programme should train around 11 000 offenders. The Department of Correctional Services has set up workshops where qualified artisans transfer skills to the participants.

The Department for Trade and Industry launched the Itukise Internships for Unemployed Graduates Programme in 2014. The programme aims to provide unemployed individuals with relevant work experience trough a 12-month internship in the private sector. In the first two years of the programme around 1 500 participants were placed in 169 companies. The NSF provides funding for the monthly stipent of the interns.

The NSF provides funding for the Sizimisele-Seto Joint Venture North West Discretionary and Innovation Project, which creates artisan training opportunities in the North West province. Training is targeted at skill needs of the province, which were identified in close co-operation with public and private sector stakeholders.

The DHET launched in mid-2012 a dual-track apprenticeship pilot, based on the successful German and Swiss apprenticeship system which combines school-based and workplace-based training in an integrated learning programme. The pilot was implemented on three sites, under the management of the Swiss-South African Cooperation Initiative, and with funding from NSF and relevant SETAs. A preliminary analysis showed that the pilot project brought value to colleges and employers, but that employers were generally reluctant to participate and that SETAs, employers and colleges faced operational problems implementing the system (Duncan, 2015).

Education and training: Policies targeting employers

In order for skills to remain relevant and up-to-date, individuals should have the opportunity to participate in training activities after leaving the formal education system. Employers should provide their employees with sufficient training options, and incentives might be needed to guarantee a sufficient offer. Additionally, sufficient workplace training places should be available for students, especially to the ones enrolled in technical and vocational training, and for unemployed individuals, as practical training is highly valued on the labour market.

Skills Development Levy

In order to incentivise employers to provide training opportunities, the 1999 Skills Development Levy Act introduced a skills levy payable by all firms with an annual wage bill of at least ZAR 500 000. The levy amounts to 1% of the total annual wage bill and must be paid to the National Revenue Fund. In the fiscal year 2014-15 ZAR 14 032 million was collected through the levy (National Treasury and SARS, 2015). From the total amount of collected skills levies, 20% is allocated to the National Skills Fund, and 80% to the SETAs. The SETAs redistribute the levy to the employers in the form of mandatory and discretionary grants (keeping 10% of the levy for administrative costs). Mandatory grants are paid to all employers that paid the levy and submitted a workplace skills plan (WPS) and annual training report (ATR). Discretionary grants are given to employers for specific training requests. Only firms eligible for the mandatory grant can request discretionary grants. Initially, employers could claim 50% of their paid levy back through the mandatory part and 20% through the discretionary funding. The regulations for the distribution of the levy through the SETAs were changed considerably in the 2012 SETA grant regulations (see Figure 3.2). The share of the mandatory grant was reduced from 50% of the levy to 20%. Furthermore, 0.5% of the levy was allocated to the Quality Council for Trades and Occupations (QCTO). The remaining funds (49.5% of the levy) are allocated to discretionary funding, but with 80% earmarked for so-called PIVOTAL grants. PIVOTAL refers to professional, vocational, technical and academic programmes that address scarce and critical skill needs. These skill needs are identified by the SETAs in their Sector Skills Plans, using information provided by the employers in their WPS and ATR. The PIVOTAL training can only be done through quality assured programmes that are registered on the National Qualifications Framework.

Figure 3.2. Skills development levy allocation

Percentage of total levy paid

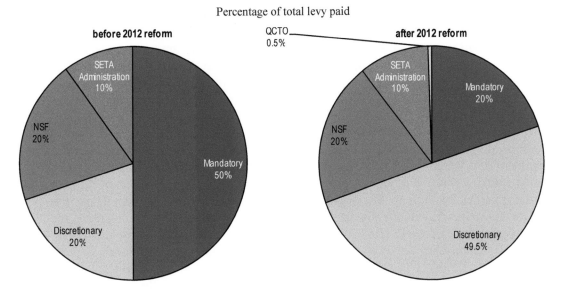

Whereas the goal of the skill development levy is to increase training opportunities at firms, the money collected through the skills levy only benefits a small number of firms. As only a small share of firms submits the WPS and ATR, many firms cannot claim the mandatory or discretionary grants. Nonetheless, as the submitting firms are generally the biggest employers, a substantial share of formal employees can potentially benefit from the grants. As a result of the low take-up of the grants, many employers see the skills levy as an additional tax. A possible reason for the low submission rate of the WPS and ATR is the administrative burden that comes with the completion of these reports, especially for smaller firms. As the reports require detailed information on employees and on provided training, as well as an assessment of skills in shortage, it can be very time-consuming for firms to complete them. While some SETAs provide support to firms in understanding how to complete the reports, for example by providing training or manuals on the use of the Organising Framework for Occupations (OFO), the process remains cumbersome. The need for a simpler process is acknowledged by the Department for Higher Education and Training, which is working on simplifying the requirements of the WPS and ATR.

The introduction of the PIVOTAL part in the discretionary grant had the goal to target spending more efficiently on the skills that are needed most in the labour market. The assessment of skill needs is based on bottom-up information from the employers combined with further analysis by the SETAs. The validity of the identified skill needs depends crucially on the quality of the information provided by employers, as well as on the capacity of the SETAs for understanding and analysing the data provided. Firms might lack the capacity to understand the skills that are needed, and especially to understand future skill needs in a changing environment. Additionally, because of the high burden put on firms in completing the ATR and WPS, they might not have the incentive to provide a detailed and researched assessment of skill needs. All SETAs use the information provided by employers to draft their Sector Skills Plans, but the methodologies differ widely. Some SETAs lack the capacities or the competencies to carry out thorough analyses.

Learnership Tax Incentive

To encourage employers to provide learnerships, the Learnership Tax Incentive was introduced in 2006. Employers get a tax refund on commencement of the learnership agreement, and a second one on completion. The amount of the refund depends on the period of the learnership agreement, the remuneration, and on whether or not the learner was already employed by the same employer when the learnerhsip started. Learnerships are work-based learning programmes that lead to a qualification that is registered in the National Qualifications Framework (NQF). A legally binding agreement between an employer, a training provider and a learner is at the basis of a learnership. Learnership programmes are managed by the SETAs. A learnership requires that a learner enter into a fixed term employment contract with the employer whilst studying towards a qualification, which is in line with the learnership (the cost of the qualification falls to the employer). Once the qualification is completed, the learnership will end, without guarantee of employment. Learnerships are available for employed and unemployed South Africans aged 16 to 35. Firms employing learners on an official learnership contract can request the tax refund from the South African Revenue Service by filing a standard tax form (IT 180 form). A review of the Learnership Tax Incentive shows that the incentive is mainly used in the finance sector, the wholesale and retail sector, and the manufacturing sector (National Treasury, 2016b). A survey of employers showed that employers value the initiative as it makes hiring and training of young (inexperienced) people more attractive. However, the respondents also signalled that there is a disconnect between the skills developed and the business needs, and that the engagement with the SETAs should be more efficient (National Treasury, 2016b).

Job creation policies

Shortages can exist because of a limited availability of individuals with the right qualifications, but even when the supply of people with the right qualification is sufficient, employers might face a shortage of *experienced* workers. The lack of experienced workers is an especially pressing problem in South Africa, where 42% of the unemployed and discouraged job seekers have never worked before (South Africa Quarterly Labour Force Survey).[2] The problem is worsened by low levels of workplace learning in the education system. According to the Anand et al. (2016), the level of experience is the most important determinant of the job-finding rate in South Africa, and especially so for youth.

Employer tax incentive

In 2014 the South African Government launched the Employer Tax Incentive, with the aim to create job opportunities for young and less experienced workers. Employers that hire a young person (age 18 to 29) can claim back the tax incentive for a period of two years. The incentive can only be reclaimed for workers earning at most ZAR 6 000 per month (and at least the minimum wage). This tax incentive can entice employers to hire more workers at a lower cost, to offer higher wages to attract workers with higher reservation wages, or to spend more on training (spending the amount of the incentive on training programmes). Take-up of the tax incentive has been high, with claims for around 130 000 jobs in 2014 and 690 000 jobs in 2015. A preliminary assessment shows that the incentive has been mainly used for the youngest cohort of the target group with low levels of experience. The incentive is more commonly used among large firms, and the biggest take-up can be seen in trade and financial and business services. The evidence suggest that the incentive has not led to job displacement in the overall workforce or among workers at the same wage level but just above the eligible age (National Treasury, 2016a).

Expanded public works programme and community works programme

In order to create job opportunities and to provide poverty and income relief for the low-skilled unemployed, the South African Department for Public Works launched the Expanded Public Works Programme (EPWP) in 2004. The participants to the project are mainly employed in public sector funded infrastructure projects, but also in the environment and culture sector, the social sector, and in non-state projects. The projects cover all spheres of government and state-owned enterprises. During the first phase of the programme (2004-09), 1.6 million work opportunities were created through the EPWP, largely exceeding the target of 1 million opportunities. In the second phase (2009-14) opportunity creation increased to 4.3 million, not reaching the target of 4.5 million (see Figure 3.3. The duration of the job opportunities in the second phase was limited to an average of 65 days. The participants were mainly unemployed individuals with some or completed secondary education, 50% of them being youth and 60% female. The third phase set a target of 6 million workplace opportunities by 2019, focussing the programme more strongly on youth.

Figure 3.3. Expanded Public Works: Job opportunities created (2004/05-2013/14)

Number of job opportunities per programme

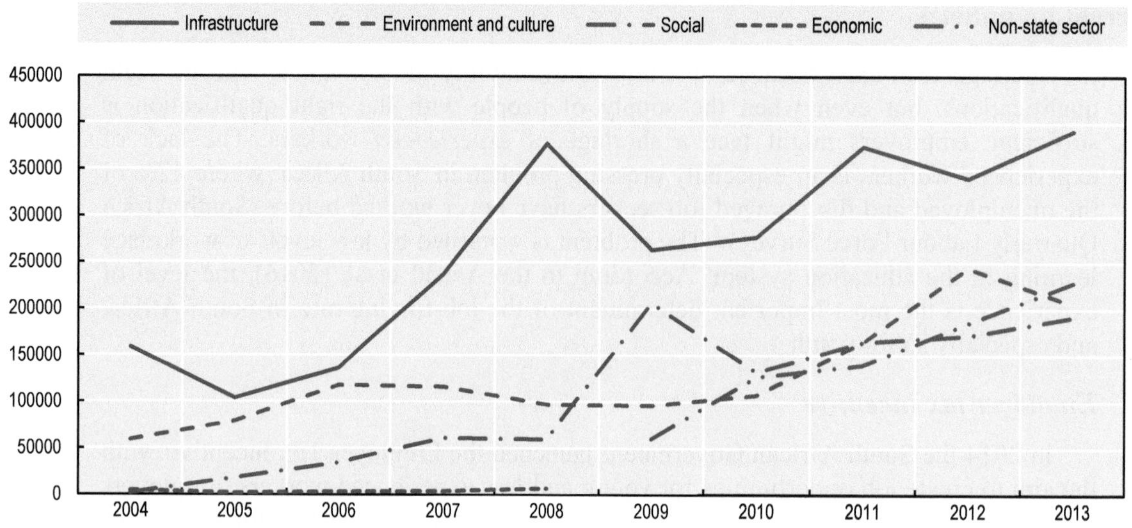

Note: Years refer to the calendar year in which the financial year started.

Source: Department of Planning, Monitoring and Evaluation (2010, 2014)

Through funding from the SETAs and DHET, the EPWP provides technical and soft skill training to some of its participants. The provided training is accredited and can take the form of occupationally-directed skills programmes, learnerships and artisan development. The first phase of the EPWP had a relatively strong focus on training. However, the targets were set too ambitiously, especially given the limited training budget, and a mid-term review showed that only 19% of the five-year target was reached after three years (HRSC, 2007). In the second phase EPWP training was refocused on training that is required to do the assigned job.

The non-state part of the EPWP was introduced in the second wave of the programme, and is mainly operationalised through the Community Works Programme (CWP). While CWP is a national programme co-ordinated by the Department of Cooperative Governance, it is implemented by non-profit agencies. The work in the CPW must be useful, defined as contributing to the public good and/or improving the quality of life in communities. The areas of useful work are identified through participatory community processes (Philip, 2013). The useful work concept is very broad, and contains areas such as food security, community care, support to early childhood development centres and to schools, and community safety. The programme is mainly implemented in rural areas, informal settlements and urban townships. The programme creates regular part-time work, without a defined limit on the duration. The CWP has been found to have positive effects on individuals, such as gained work experience and increased household food security, and on communities (Centre for Democratising Information, 2013a). Communities have benefited in the form of improved learning environments in primary schools, lower levels of crime and stronger social cohesion, but the impact crucially depends in the integrity of implementation (Centre for Democratising Information, 2013b; Langa et al., 2016).

> ## Box 3.4. Private sector and regional government initiatives for work experience creation
>
> ### EOH Youth Job Creation Initiative
>
> EOH, a South African company providing ICT consulting, systems integration and outsourcing, encourages private sector companies to provide learnerships and internships for young South Africans. By providing information and practical advice on the existing financial incentives, such as the skills development levy and the learnership tax incentive, EOH engages its clients and business partners to create opportunities for youth to develop valuable work experience. Furthermore, within this initiative, EOH also co-operates with education and training institutions and SETAs. The initiative was endorsed by multiple government departments. To set the example, EOH has launched multiple waves of their internal learnership programme, bringing on board 600 learners and graduate interns in each wave, of which 75% to 80% were appointed official EOH positions after the completion of the programme.
>
> ### Western Cape's Work & Skills programme
>
> The Work and Skills for 100 000 Programme is an in 2009 launched initiative of the Western Cape Government targeted at the unemployed of the region. The main focus group are the unemployed youth who have achieved a Matric or equivalent qualification and have been out of school for at least one year. The majority of the participants should be from rural areas in the province. The programme aims to reduce poverty and unemployment through the provision of temporary work experience, which increases the employment and self-employment prospects of the participants. The programme intents to create 100 000 jobs with learning opportunities over a period of five years in the Western Cape's economic and social sectors. These job opportunities will be provided by the private and public sector. Potential learners undergo general and/or company specific entry assessments to optimise the match between learner and employer. Participants to the programme get a monthly stipend (subsidised by the Western Cape Government, and potentially topped-up by the private sector employer) and are assigned a mentor. In the first three years of the programme, about 3 000 individuals participated in the programme.

Migration policies

Education and training are not the only channels to increase the supply of skills in demand. Attracting skilled workers from abroad is another possibility which can be particularly interesting when the need for skills is urgent, when training programmes are long, or when the necessary training programmes are not yet in place.

General Work Visa

When employers are unable to find someone with the right skills for a job opening, they can recruit someone from outside South Africa on a General Work Visa. Before such a visa can be granted, the employer must show that sufficient efforts were made to recruit a local suitable candidate, and that the search was unsuccessful. Generally, this means that the job opening must be advertised in a national newspaper, and that applicants whose qualifications and experience correspond to the vacancy have to be interviewed. The employer must provide proof of the job advertisement to the Department of Labour, as well as details of the applicants and reasons why they were not suitable for the job. Based on the submitted evidence, the Department of Labour submits a positive or negative letter of recommendation to the Department of Home Affairs. When a job fulfils the criteria to be filled by a foreign candidate, i.e. when a positive letter of recommendation is issued, the foreign national receiving the job offer must prove that he has the right skills, experience and qualifications for the job.

Critical Skill Visa

To attract foreigners with skills that are in shortage in South Africa, the Department of Home Affairs introduced the Quota Work Permit in 2002, which was replaced by the Critical Skill Visa in 2014. Individuals with skills that feature on the Critical Skills list published by the Department of Home Affairs can apply for a Critical Skills Visa. This list is based on the DHET list of occupations in high demand, focussing mainly on higher-skilled occupations. The department of Home Affairs consults with experts and labour representatives on the occupations that should or should not be on the list. The list that is currently in force dates back to 2014.

The main difference between the Critical Skills Visa and the General Work Visa is that employers do not have to prove that they did a diligent search for South African labour to fill the position before offering it a foreigner. Another important difference between the two types of visa is that family members of foreigners with a critical skills visa can take up any type of employment in South Africa, whereas family members of individuals on a General Work Visa are restricted from working in South Africa. Finally, the Critical Skills Visa can also be granted to foreign individuals without a job offering in South Africa. In that case the initial visa is limited to a 12-month period, during which employment has to be secured in order to get a renewal. While the former system (Quota Work Permit) set limits on the number of foreigners with critical skills that could be awarded the visa, the number of entrants under the current system is unlimited.

Notes

1. The only requirements to participate in the National Senior Certificate for Adults examination is to have i) an official grade 9 school report which indicates promotion to grade 10, ii) a general education or training certificate for adults, or iii) another SAQA-registered NQF level 2 or 3 qualification with a language and mathematics as fundamentals.

2. The 2015 South African Labour Force Survey show that 38.8% of unemployed individuals never worked. Among discouraged job-seekers, defined as persons who wanted to work but did not try to find work or start a business because they believed that there were no jobs available in their area, or were unable to find jobs requiring their skills, or they had lost hope of finding any kind of work, this share reaches 47.8%.

References

Anand, R., S. Kothari and N. Kumar (2016), "South Africa: Labor Market Dynamics and Inequality", *IMF Working Paper*, No. 16/137.

Centre for Democratising Information (2013a), "The South African Community Capability Study: The Community Work Programme".

Centre for Democratising Information (2013b), "The South African Community Capability Study: The context of public primary education and the Community Work Programme".

DHET (2014), *Statistics on Post-School Education and Training in South Africa* 2014, Pretoria.

DHET (2013), "Report of the Ministerial Committee on the Review of the National Student Financial Aid Scheme".

Duncan, K. (2015), "Piloting Dual-track Apprenticeships in South Africa", *African Journal for Work-Based Learning*, Vol. 3, pp. 78-91.

Gunning, D., J. Van Kleef and P. Werquin (2008), "Recognition of Non-formal and Informal Learning: Country Note for South Africa", OECD Publishing, Paris.

Harambee (2017), "Breaking Barriers", *Quarterly Employment Report*, first quarter 2017.

HRSC (2007), "Mid-term Feview of the Expanded Public Works Programme: Synthesis Report", *HRSC Research Report*.

Langa, M. et al. (2016), "Facilitating or Hindering Social Cohesion? The Impact of the Community Work Programme in selected South African Townships", *SA Crime Quarterly*, No. 55.

Makeketa, J. and M.C. Maphalala (2014), "Recognition of Prior Learning: Are We Bridging the Gap Between Policy and Practice in the Workplace?, *Mediterranean Journal of Social Sciences*, Vol. 5, No. 1.

Marock, C. (2000), "Prior learning: What and Why?", *South African Labour Bulletin*, Vol. 24, No. 2.

National Treasury (2016a), *Employment Tax Incentive Descriptive Report*, National Treasury, Pretoria.

National Treasury (2016b), *Learnership Tax Incentive Review*, Pretoria.

National Treasury and SARS (2015), *2015 Tax Statistics*, National Treasury and SARS, Pretoria.

NSFAS (2015), *2014/15 Annual Report: NSFAS Towards a Student-centred Approach*, NSFAS, Cape Town.

OECD (2010), *Recognising Non-Formal and Informal Learning: Outcomes, Policies and Practices*, OECD Publishing, Paris, http://dx.doi.org/10.1787/9789264063853-en.

Philip, K. (2013), "The Community Work Programme: Building a Society that Works", *ILO Employment Working Paper*, No. 149.

Chapter 4

Challenges and recommendations for South Africa

In spite of the extensive range of policy initiatives to tackle skills imbalances in South Africa, some challenges remain. This chapter zooms in on the most important challenges, and provides recommendations that can be used by public and private stakeholders to improve the skills outcomes of the country. Best practice examples from other countries are provided to illustrate how policies can effectively address skills imbalances. These recommendations and examples can guide South African policy-makers in the (re-)design of new and existing policies to reduce skills shortages, surpluses and mismatch.

Poor quality and limited use of skill needs data

The identification of skills and occupations in shortage in South Africa relies to a large extent on the Sector Skills Plans (SSP) issued by the SETAs. The shortages identified by the SETAs feed, together with data from other sources, into the list of occupations in high demand, and are used as the basis for allocating the PIVOTAL funds. SETAs differ widely in how they determine shortages in their sector, as they can freely choose which method and which data to use for this exercise. As a result, the quality of shortage assessment exercises will rely heavily on the data analysis capacity of the SETAs. Furthermore, to correctly anticipate skill needs, SETAs have to understand the longer-term trends in their sector. Given the big differences in SETA performance, it is likely that the quality of the skills assessment outcomes differs widely between SETAs. While the DHET has developed an outline of the SSP, with five chapters that SETAs have to include, SETAs are free to choose the topics to discuss within each chapter. To help SETAs develop optimal SSPs, DHET has provided suggestions for content of each chapter, based on set of key questions. Additionally, DHET provides support to SETA in terms of annual capacity building workshops, one-to-one sessions and sessions with clusters of SETAs. To ensure a certain level of quality of the SSPs, DHET reviews a draft of the plan on completeness, as well as the use of research methods and stakeholder involvement. In 2011 a Ministerial Task Team on SETA Performance was created, which published recommendations on improving the SETA performance. To ensure better skills planning using SETA-collected data, the Task Team recommended restricting the role of SETAs in skills planning to data collection, and entrusting the data analysis to a national central body.

The quality of the Sector Skills Plans does not only depend on the SETAs, but also on the underlying data used for the exercise. The Sector Skill Plans use data provided by the employers in their Workplace Skill Plans and Annual Training Reports. However, with a large share of employers, especially SMEs, not submitting their WSP and ATR, the data used to assess shortages are not representative of the full population of employers. Aside from not being fully representative, the data can potentially also be of low quality, when employers are not fully engaged in providing high quality information. As employers often see the submission of their WSP as an act of compliance, rather than an act to help them assess their skill needs and optimise their labour inputs, there is a risk of them not putting sufficient resources or effort into the submission. For employers to be able to get the mandatory grant, their WSP has to be approved by the SETA, as such introducing an element of quality assurance. However, it is difficult to verify the quality of the submissions, and SETAs often lack the capacity to do this. The 2013 White Paper on Post-School Education and Training acknowledges the issues of data collection through the WSPs, and the DHET is currently working on simplifying and standardising the templates for the WSPs, as a means to improve quantity and quality of submissions. In developing the new WSP template, the results from the pilot SETA Labour Market Survey should be analysed thoroughly, including the satisfaction of respondents.

Other countries have used uniform employer surveys to detect recruitment difficulties. In the United Kingdom, for example, the Migration Advisory Committee (MAC) uses information on vacancies provided directly by employers through the National Employer Survey. They construct three indicators at the occupational level to assess whether an occupation is in shortage or not: i) percentage of skill-shortage vacancies relative to employment, ii) percentage of skill-shortage vacancies relative to all vacancies, and iii) percentage of skill-shortage vacancies relative to hard-to-fill vacancies. When these indicators exceed a certain threshold they are said to indicate a shortage. A similar consistent methodology could be used in South Africa, if SETAs were to ask employers to share data about the number of vacancies they are facing (all, hard-to-fill, skill-shortage) and if all SETAs used the same threshold level to identify shortages. This survey could be based on the SETA Labour Market Survey, taking into account the possible issues that were detected during its pilot phase.

Currently, only a limited number of South African employers analyse and evaluate their skill needs on a regular basis. When employers understand their existing and future skill needs, they can better anticipate and plan their training and hiring decisions. While firms are currently encouraged to undertake skill need exercises through the skill levy system, further incentives might be needed, especially for smaller firms. In France, for example, large firms (of at least 300 employees) are required to do an analysis of their skill needs at least once every three years, and negotiate on the required actions with the social partners. While the requirement does not hold for smaller firms, government funded financial aid is available for small firms wanting to do a skill need exercise.

Whereas the critical skills lists of the SETAs are mainly for internal use (i.e. for PIVOTAL grant allocation), the list of occupations in high demand, compiled by DHET, aims to be a tool for policy makers and the wider public. The list is used by the Department of Home Affairs to develop its list of critical skills for issuing Critical Skills Visa. DHET also uses the list to provide career guidance, through specialised leaflets and their career advice portal (NCAP). While the list is published on the DHET website, and as such made available to a wide public, it is not very user-friendly. The document containing the list can be downloaded from the website, and gives a plain overview of all the occupations in high demand, as well as a discussion of the methodology. In order to make the list more accessible to a wider audience, it could be made more interactive. In Finland, for example, the shortage information (*Ammattibarometri*) is available as a comprehensive list with colour coding for the degree of shortage (per region), as interactive maps with data on unemployment and vacancies, as a summary poster and as a shorter version of top 15 occupations. Additionally, for the South African list to be more useful to a range of stakeholders, it could link the occupations in high demand to the actual skills that are required in those occupations. The occupational information website in Sweden (*Yrkeskompassen*) contains, in addition to information on expected shortages, detailed information about education and training options and requirements for each occupation, as well as the associated skills or abilities.

While the DHET list of occupations in high demand provides information on shortages at the national level, and the SETA scarce skills lists provide information at the sectoral level, South Africa misses skill need information at the regional level. The large majority of OECD countries have regional level skills assessments, either as part of the national assessment or as an individual regional assessment (OECD, 2016). In Canada, for example, the skills shortage assessment exercise that is done at the national level, using labour force data, is repeated at the regional level. The assessment is slightly adjusted to reflect that labour force data at the regional level is less reliable because of smaller sample sizes. Additionally, the Canadian regions have their own shortage assessment systems. The province of British Columbia, for example, uses labour force data in combination with stakeholder input to draw up its High Opportunity Occupations List. Given the substantial economic and labour market differences between South African provinces, a skill needs assessment at the provincial level could be valuable.

Box 4.1. Recommendations: Quality and use of skill need data

- Develop a uniform method for SETAs to identify skill needs. Provide training and support to SETAs who lack the capacity to implement this method. Alternatively, the skill needs assessment exercises could be centralised and executed by a body with strong statistical capacity.

- Rather than relying on the information from the WSPs, narrowly-defined and easily measurable employer information on (hard-to-fill) vacancies should be used. This information can be collected through a survey of a representative sample of firms. In order not to overburden employers, the questions can be added to an already existing employer survey, such as the Quarterly Employment Survey.

- If the annual WSP would disappear, firms should still be encouraged to undertake reviews of their existing and future skill needs. Additional support can be given to SMEs to implement these exercises.

- The list of occupations in high demand should be distributed widely to all relevant stakeholders. To facilitate the use of the list, a dedicated webpage should be setup, which is user-friendly and provide more information on the shortage occupations. The webpage should have an easy search function and occupations should have links to the required qualifications (possibly on the NCAP website) and job openings (through the PES). This webpage should be easy to find, and other relevant government departments or agencies, such as the PES, should refer to it.

Quality of education

The South African labour market is characterised by a large surplus of low-skilled workers, with many low-skilled individuals in (long-term) unemployment. A large share of South-Africans has below upper-secondary education, and while this share is lower among younger cohorts, it remains substantial. This relatively high share of individuals who did not finish upper secondary education can be attributed to large numbers of students dropping out between grade 10 and grade 12, as well as students not passing the Matric test at the end of grade 12 (70.7% pass rate in 2015). To pass the Matric exam, a student must score at least 40% in three subjects (including an official language at home language level) and 30% in the remaining four subjects. The high dropout rate, low Matric pass rate and low passing requirements are all symptoms of low quality basic education in South Africa.[1] This low quality is reflected in the low scores of South African students in international standard tests (e.g. TIMMS). Low quality basic education is linked to, among others, low teacher quality, teacher shortages, poor infrastructure and lack of resources (Murtin, 2013). Substantial differences exists between schools, with historically disadvantaged school, mainly located in rural areas and townships, often facing important resource constraints limiting the quality of education they can offer. Other countries have been able to improve their overall educational quality and reduce between-school disparities over a relatively short period of time by implementing a comprehensive set of reforms (e.g. Poland, see Box 4.3). While many challenges remain, evidence from international tests show significant improvements in the quality of South African basic education over the last years (Gustafsson, 2017).

Vocational education in South Africa is also generally perceived as being of low quality, which can potentially explain why labour market outcomes of diploma or certificate holders are significantly worse than those of individuals with university degrees – although being above the country-wide average (van Broekhuizen, 2016).[2] Teachers in TVET colleges lack practical knowledge, and subjects and technologies are often outdated. In an attempt to modernise vocational education, DHET introduced the National Certificate Vocational (NCV) programmes in 2007, while phasing out the older National Accredited Technical Education Diploma (Nated) vocational programmes. The reform was, however, unsuccessful with high dropout rates and employers complaining about the lack of workplace training, and the Nated courses were reintroduced. Whereas vocational training should prepare students for working life, employers report that vocational graduates lack necessary workplace skills and experience. The lack of (relevant) work experience among graduates is linked to the low availability of workplace training places for learnerships. While the discretionary part of the skills development levy can be used for funding learnerships, and special tax incentives have been developed, further incentives for employers might be necessary to create sufficient workplace learning opportunities. Strong employer involvement in the design of learnerships, like in Germany (Box 4.3), can improve their quality and availability.

The share of individuals with tertiary degrees in South Africa is low. This is linked to the low number of high-school students obtaining the pass mark to enter university, but also to the large number of eligible students not entering tertiary education and a high dropout rate. Recent estimates suggest that about one third of students with a bachelor pass do not enter university, and that about 30% of entrants drop out before graduating (van Broekhuizen et al., 2016). Low throughput and high dropout are likely to be linked to the relative soft entry requirements for higher education, but also to limit capacity of higher education institutions and a lack of financial support. In order to limit financial constraints for university participation, the provision of student loans could be increased. Bridging courses could potentially help reduce dropout and increase the skill level of graduates.

Box 4.2. Recommendations: Education quality

Basic education

- Encourage students to choose teaching as a career, by making the teaching profession more attractive. At the same time, increase the quality of teacher training. Provide additional incentives for teachers to teach in historically disadvantaged schools.

- Provide tailored career advice to students early on in the schooling system to reduce dropout, increase throughput to further education and improve labour market outcomes. As South African students make important subject choices at young ages, it is important for them to be well-informed about possible career paths. Career counselling should be an integral part of teacher training. Moreover, advice should be linked to the student's abilities, which should be assessed thoroughly before students make subject choices that influence their further study path. A re-introduction of standardised tests, especially at the end of general education, could be considered. Particular attention should be given to science and math subjects.

- Develop clear pathways to vocational and occupational programmes after grade 9. A grade 9 certificate could help students without Matric access these programmes.

- Ensure sufficient and effective government spending on education. Private sector players should be encouraged to develop education funding initiatives both at the school and post-school level.

- Assure quality of education through regular school and class inspections, including teacher evaluations. Additionally, quality can be monitored through standardised tests.

Further and higher education

- Provide sufficient financial opportunities for students to access further and higher education, through loans and bursaries. Spending on bursaries could be targeted on fields with the highest degree of skill needs.

- As long as the quality of basic education is unsatisfactory, further and higher education institutions should provide (non-compulsory) bridging programmes to first year students in order to increase their foundational skills, and student should be encouraged to participate in these programmes. This could contribute to lower drop-out rates and higher overall skills of graduates.

- Better align the vocational education system to practices and needs in the workplace. Teachers should be involved in continuous training, to keep their skills up to date. The training offer and content should be responsive to local needs, and employers should be involved in every step of the TVET value chain. Vocational programmes should not be too specific to give graduates access to a wide range of employment opportunities.

- Employers should provide more workplace training opportunities for vocational students. By reducing the administrative burden for firms, especially SMEs, on applying for funding under the skills development levy system, more firms could be willing to offer training places. Employers providing workplace training should assign trained mentors to learners. Further promoting the learnership tax incentive could also increase the number of training places.

- Closely monitor and evaluate the outcomes of different education paths. This information can be used to redesign the offer and content of different programmes, and for career guidance purposes. Tracer studies would be a good tool for measuring outcomes.

Box 4.3. Education quality: International best practices

Basic and secondary education: Poland's improvement in PISA test scores

When Poland first participated in the OECD's international student assessment PISA in 2000, it ranked below the OECD average in terms of reading, mathematics and science. Since then the country's PISA scores gradually improved, and by 2009 its scores were above the OECD average for all subjects. This was driven by a reduction in the number of low-performing students and an increase in the number of high-performing students. The country also substantially reduced the between-school variation in student performance. Poland's improvement in PISA scores has been much stronger than the trend observed in other participating transition economies.

The significant improvement in educational quality in Poland is linked to the substantial education reforms that were implemented starting in 1999 (World Bank, 2010; OECD, 2011; Zawistowska, 2014). The most important elements of the reforms were a delayed tracking into vocational streams, a greater number of hours spent on language instruction, the introduction of externally evaluated examinations at the end of every stage of education, changes in the pay structure of teachers, and the decentralisation of curriculum development to the local level, while keeping curricular standards at the national level.

Vocational education: The German "dual" apprenticeship system

In Germany, high-school students can choose at the end of compulsory education to pursue academic upper secondary education or to follow a vocational path. The vocational path can be done at full-time vocational schools or in the dual apprenticeship system. In 2014, 48% of German upper-secondary students were enrolled in vocational programmes, of which 86% in the dual-based system (*OECD Education Database*). Vocational education and training is widely respected in the German society.

Students in the dual system divide their time between workplace training and training at vocational schools. Students spend 12 hours per week at school, receiving both general education and occupation-specific education. Employers, through the Economic Chambers, have a strong role in vocational education, being involved in curriculum preparation and supervising the provision of workplace training. The high degree of engagement and ownership of employers in the dual system is complemented with a strong government involvement, guaranteeing that the educational and economic goals of the system are not hindered by short-term needs of the employers. To ensure quality, the government develops standardised, binding national training curricula which are updated regularly. Job quality is guaranteed through apprenticeship contracts with collectively agreed wages. Because of the strong employer involvement, vocational programmes can easily adapt to local needs. Funding of the dual system is split between employers and government (OECD, 2010).

The success of the German vocational model is linked to its long history and the fact that it is well-rooted in the German society. Therefore, simply copying the German system in other countries will not guarantee success. The system should be adapted to the economic, social and educational context of the country, and potentially only parts of the German system should be introduced (Euler, 2013).

Source: OECD (2010), *Recognising Non-formal and Informal Learning: Outcomes, Policies and Practices*, OECD Publishing, Paris; Euler, D. (2013), *Germany's Dual Vocational Training System: A Model for Other Countries?*, Bertelsmann Stiftung, Gütersloh; OECD (2011), "The Impact of the 1999 Education Reform in Poland", *OECD Education Working Papers*, No. 49; World Bank (2010), "Successful Education Reforms: Lessons from Poland", *World Bank Knowledge Brief*, Vol. 34; Zawistowska, A. (2014), "The Black Box of the Educational Reforms in Poland: What Caused the Improvement in the PISA Scores of Polish Students", *Polish Sociological Review*, No. 3.

Access to and availability of lifelong learning opportunities

The skills development levy was introduced to incentivise employers to provide training for their employees. However, by construction, the levy system excludes very small firms, as well as informal employers. Additionally, as a result of the high administrative burden faced by firms for reclaiming funding through the levy system, many firms, especially SMEs, do not access this form of funding. Access to learning opportunities through the levy funding system is therefore generally limited to employees of big firms. Subsidies for training targeted at SMEs have been implemented in many countries, like Australia and Mexico (Box 4.5).

The largest part of the available discretionary grants under the skills development levy system is earmarked for PIVOTAL training. Whereas the focus of funding on the development of skills that are in high demand is a positive development, with a likely positive impact on the reduction of skills imbalances, the restriction on the type of training might be too tight. The PIVOTAL funding only covers training programmes that are registered on the NQF, quality assured, and lead to (part) qualifications. As a result of the focus on formal and generally longer-term training, the lowest-skilled might not be able to participate. Also, many valuable training programmes are not registered on the NQF.

Recognition of Prior Learning (RPL) is an important tool for individuals to get the skills acquired on the job accredited with a formal qualification. This is especially relevant for people who did not obtain a formal degree in the education system. Obtaining a formal degree through RPL can increase labour mobility of workers, both between employers, but also between jobs at the same employer (career advancement). While South Africa has had an RPL system in place for many years, it has not been used optimally. The awareness of the system and its potential benefits for workers is relatively low, and participation in RPL activities by the lowest-skilled is restricted by the form of RPL, which generally requires a certain level of literacy skills. Recognition of learning could go beyond hard skills, as was recently done in France with the introduction of a certificate for acquired soft skills (Box 4.5).

Many of the training policies in South Africa are targeted at people in employment, while the unemployed are often overlooked. One of the key drivers of the National Skills Fund is to meet the training needs of the unemployed, but the NSF has been lacking clear focus. SETAs can fund training for the unemployed, but there are no rules governing this. The South African PES can only provide information on possible education or training to the unemployed, as the Department of Labour has no responsibilities in training matters. As South Africa has a large pool of low-skilled unemployed, there is a huge training need. Other countries, like New Zealand and France, provide subsidies to employers for hiring and training unemployed individuals (Box 4.5). The EPWP, which reaches a large group of low-skilled unemployed, has only a very limited training component. While the EPWP does create some work experience for the unemployed, and contributes to poverty alleviation, without skills development component the programme is unlikely to significantly increase the work opportunities of the unemployed after exiting the EPWP. Ideally, EPWP participation would result in the development of new skills or the improvement of existing skills, which could potentially be recognised through RPL.

South African adults who lack basic skills have the opportunity to enrol in Adult Basic Education Centres to obtain those critical skills. With a substantial part of the South African population not having finished upper secondary education, the need for such second chance education opportunities is pressing. Whereas the focus of publicly provided Adult education is the past has been foundational skills, the shift towards the new Community Colleges opens the curricula to broader components, which should address local skill needs. As the ultimate goal of adult education is to equip adults with skills to access a decent living, extending the programme from basic skills to other useful skills, such as technical skills or entrepreneurial skills, is a welcome evolution.

Box 4.4. Recommendations: Lifelong learning

- Encourage and provide support to small firms for getting access to training under the skills development levy system. This could be done by lowering the administrative burden faced by firms for getting access to funds. Additional tax incentives or subsidies could be made available for SMEs.

- Make the provisions for PIVOTAL training more flexible, such that employers can more easily access training to suits their needs. Training options should remain restricted to areas of skill needs, and quality assurance remains essential.

- Promote the use of RPL among employees and employers, as well as the unemployed. Make sure the mode of assessment is flexible, such that is tailored to the specific situation of the individual. Ensure that employees are supported by their employer during the process, e.g. in terms of time to work on their portfolio. PES workers should actively recommend RPL to the unemployed, and should provide assistance throughout the recognition process. RPL could go beyond hard skills and formal qualifications, and also recognise soft skills that are valued by employers.

- Scale up the efforts for training of the unemployed. Both SETAs and the NSF should allocate sufficient resources to the unemployed, and the funds should prioritise training for skills in high demand. Not only should the PES provide information on training, but they could become a one-stop-shop where unemployed can register for training that suits their needs. As such, the PES should work closely with the SETAs, the NSF and community colleges, but also with private sector training providers (e.g. NGOs). These PES services should not be restricted to unemployed individuals eligible for benefits, as this tends to excludes first-time job seekers and re-entrants such as youth and women.

- The Community College plan should be rolled out as soon as possible. Consultation with local stakeholders, like employers and NGOs, has to be implemented to guarantee that the educational offer corresponds to local needs. Co-operation with NGOs already active in adult and youth training could speed up the process and could provide useful insights. Successful non-public adult training centers could be incorporated in the Community College system by classifying them as official delivery sites.

- The National Skills Fund should be made more transparent, and its funding projects should be more focused on the development of critical skills. The funds should largely benefit the most disadvantaged groups, including the unemployed.

Box 4.5. Training for the employed and unemployed: Best practices

Hiring and training the unemployed in New Zealand and France

In New Zealand employers can get government support when they hire someone who is on unemployment benefits and needs extra training to do the job. The government will pay the wage of the new hire for a period up to one year while being in training, and the cost of training. Employers only qualify for this subsidy when they hire the unemployed individual on a permanent job of at least 30 hours per week, paying the market wage. Employers also have to show that no employees were dismissed to employ to unemployed individual.

Similarly, in France the public employment services covers (part of) the cost of 400 training hours as well as the wage of unemployed individuals that are being hired and trained. Training can be provided internally or externally, and a higher ceiling on hourly training cost repayment is set for externally provided training. This programme, the *Préparation Opérationnelle à l'Emploi*, only covers the unemployed who are hired on a permanent contract or on a fixed-term contract of at least 12 months. However, similar subsidies exist for certain contracts of shorter duration (*Action de Formation Préalable au Recrutement*).

Training the employed in Australia and Mexico

To support SMEs in their ability to grow and succeed in a rapidly changing economy, Australia set up the Industry Skills Fund. Funding is available for SMEs in priority industries to invest in training of their employees. SMEs can also receive skills advice, which should help them understand their growth opportunity and identify the skills needed to increase their competitiveness. Larger businesses can also participate, although a smaller share of their training costs will be covered. Firms in non-priority industries can only receive assistance from the Industry Skills Fund when they demonstrate that they have significant growth potential and are ready to take advantage of economic opportunities.

Since 1988 the Integral Quality and Modernization Program (CIMO, later renamed PAC) has provided subsidised training for Mexican SMEs. The programme initially focussed solely on training, but its scope was broadened over the years as it was recognised that a lack of training was only one of the many factors that contributes to low productivity among SMEs. Training and technical assistance is provided by public and private providers, usually on a group basis to lower the cost. Firms that are interested in participating in PAC first undergo a diagnostic by PAC promoters to identify production methods, skills and other firm-specific constraints. They then receive training and other technical assistance tailored specifically to their needs on a cost-sharing basis. The programme proactively identifies and engages SMEs using its decentralised network of Training Promotion Units located in local associations and chambers of commerce. Empirical evidence suggests that CIMO/PAC has generally been effective in increasing the performance of SMEs, through – amongst others – increased investment in worker training.

Recognition and improvement of soft skills in France

To help individuals who do not have any formal qualification, but possess relevant basic skills, France developed the CléA certificate. This certificate should help unemployed individuals in finding a job, and should assist employed individuals in their career progress. To obtain the certificate candidates (employed or unemployed individuals) can get in touch with a CléA contact point, which assesses the candidate's skills in seven domains. These domains are expression, calculation and/or discussion, the use of a computer, following rules and teamwork, working independently and taking initiatives, willingness to learn, and mastering basic rules (safety, environment, hygiene). If the candidate lacks the necessary skills in one or more of these domains, a personalised training plan is made, such that these skills can be brought up to speed. Training is generally provided through short-term and practical programmes. Once a candidate obtains the necessary skill level in all domains, the certificate can be granted by a jury.

Source: OECD (2017). *Getting Skills Right: Financial Incentives for Steering Education and Training Acquisition*, OECD Publishing, Paris; Tan, H. and G. Lopez Acevedo (2005), "Evaluation Training Programmes for Small and Medium Enterprises: Lessons from Mexico", *World Bank Policy Research Paper*, No. 3760.

Co-ordination between stakeholders

In order for policies to be effective at tackling skills shortages and mismatch in South Africa, they must cover a wide range of different areas. Shortages and mismatch must be addressed both from the supply and from the demand side. As such, different departments, such as Basic Education, DHET, Trade and Industry, Small Business Development, the Department of Labour and the Department of Home Affairs, should be co-operating to tackle the issues. In South Africa, government departments very often work in silos, with too little co-operation or co-ordination between them. A key example is the NSDS, which is developed by DHET, without any involvement with the Department for Basic Education. Similarly, while career guidance is located in DHET, there should be close co-operation with the Department of Basic Education, as career advice should be given early on in life. Strategies for improving labour market outcomes, including the operations of the PES, are strongly linked to education and training policies, and therefore co-operation between the Department of Labour and DHET and the Department for Basic Education is crucial. The need for better co-ordination between government departments was also highlighted by Reddy et al. (2016) in their analysis of skills supply and demand.

To understand skill needs, policy makers need to have an understanding of what is going on at the employer-level. Employers are facing the realities of shortages and mismatch, and are therefore best placed to provide input on skill needs. Employers in South Africa generally complain that they are not enough involved in policy development. While the business side is generally asked to provide feedback on policy drafts, they deem consultation to happen at a too late stage, limiting their potential impact. SETAs or employer organisations should be the link between policy makers and employers.

In order for the education and training offer and content to be responsive to skill needs, there has to be strong co-operation between employers and training providers. As it is difficult for training providers to understand the ongoing trends on the demand side, they should be in close contact with employers. Good relations between these two parties could potentially also lead to a higher willingness of firms to offer workplace training places. SETAs are best placed to serve as an intermediary between employers and training providers, but generally they have not done sufficiently in this role. In the Sector Skills Plans SETAs have to analyse their existing relationships and identify gaps. This exercise serves as a good first step in the evaluation of the SETAs' role and performance. Training providers, from their side, must understand the importance of being responsive to the needs of employers. The government should facilitate co-ordination and co-operation by providing a platform for interaction, possibly at the SETA level.

Strong communication between employers and employees can help firms better understand their existing skills imbalances and training requirements. Furthermore, a good relationship between employers and employees might result in an increased willingness of employers to provide training opportunities and a higher participation rate of employees. Labour relations in South Africa are generally viewed as confrontational, and a recent survey ranks South Africa last among 118 countries in terms of the quality of labour-employer co-operation (INSEAD, 2016).

Box 4.6. Recommendations: Co-ordination between stakeholders

- Improve co-operation across government departments. Strategies and policies should involve all relevant departments sharing efforts to reach agreed targets. Co-ownership of strategies and policies is encouraged. Co-ordination with other departments should happen at an early stage.

- Employers should voice their ideas and concerns on skills policies to policy makers, ideally through existing bodies like SETAs or employer organisations. The input from employers should be taken on board early in the policy development process. Trust between employers and government should be improved.

- The relationship between employers and training providers should be strengthened and improved, possibly by strengthening the role of the SETAs as intermediaries and by creating platforms for co-operation. This will give a chance to employers to communicate directly with training providers on local skill needs. By creating close links with employers, training institutions would find it easier to accommodate demand for workplace learning. Co-operation between SETA and training providers could be encouraged by aligning the government funding agreements

---

Lack of or poor implementation of policies

The myriad of strategies addressing skills issues clearly shows that tackling skills imbalances is high on the policy agenda in South Africa. While these documents generally set out strategic objectives to tackle the skills issues, a clear framework for implementing the strategy and ultimately fulfilling the objectives is often not provided. The strategies could put forward measurable short-term and long-term targets to be used for monitoring and evaluation purposes. In this framework, progress would be monitored on a regular basis. In addition, feasible targets would need to be set, in order to make the strategy a credible tool for tackling skills issues and not to discourage stakeholders. On the other hand, targets should also not be too easy to reach, as the goal of the strategy is to lead to significant improvements, rather than only making minor changes. Ideally, strategies identify the key players for delivering each of the objectives, and sufficient resources are allocated to reaching these objectives.

In order for policies, and especially strategies, to be implemented successfully, the relevant stakeholders need to understand and support the policies. Skills policies and strategies generally touch upon a large set of stakeholders, and their engagement is detrimental for a successful implementation. A sense of ownership would need to be created in order for stakeholders to feel involved and accept to contribute. This should already be done early on in the policy development process, by allowing stakeholders to voice their opinion on the problem and provide policy suggestions, and involve them actively in the policy drafting stage. Stakeholders should also be involved in monitoring and evaluation exercises, to understand possible implementation issues and areas for improvement.

It generally takes time before policies or strategies are fully implemented, and working optimally. While policies should be flexible in order to respond to possible design or implementation issues, and to changing economic circumstances, guaranteeing the stability of policies is also important. When political powers change, it is important to maintain stability of policies. While drastic changes to policies and continuous adoption of new strategies make the system overly complex, they can also lead to a loss of stakeholder engagement.

4. CHALLENGES AND RECOMMENDATIONS FOR SOUTH AFRICA– **71**

Box 4.7. Recommendations: Policy implementation

- Set measurable targets in strategic documents in order to facilitate monitoring and evaluation. These targets should be based on research, and should be set at ambitious but not unfeasible levels. To ensure engagement in reaching the targets, stakeholders should be actively involved in the target-setting process. Overall, stakeholders should be involved during each step of policy making in order to provide a sense of ownership

- Evaluate the measures put in place to ensure that they are delivering the intended results in a cost-effective way. To the extent possible and, where applicable, robust evaluations using experimental methods should be privileged when introducing new policies.

- Ensure that policies and strategies are not too sensitive to the political cycle. Well-designed policies and strategies should not disappear or be changed dramatically every time the political power changes.

Notes

1. Other factors that have been identified as potentially contributing to poor education outcomes in South Africa include the quality of early childhood development (Ilifa Labantwana, Children's Institute and DPME, 2016) and the mismatch between home language and language of learning and teaching (Department of Basic Education, 2010).

2. It is not easy to make the distinction between TVET college graduates and higher education institution (HEI) graduates in existing South African survey data. Van Broekhuizen (2016) compares diploma and certificate holders, which can be both TVET and HEI graduates, to university degree holders, which can only be HEI graduates. He argues that the former group consists for a large part of TVET graduates, and that the labour market outcomes of this group will be strongly influenced by these TVET graduates.

References

Department of Basic Education (2010), "The Status of the Language of Learning and Teaching (LOLT) in Schools: A Quantitative Overview", Department of Basic Education, Pretoria.

Euler, D. (2013), *Germany's Dual Vocational Training System: A Model for Other Countries?*, Bertelsmann Stiftung, Gütersloh.

Gustafsson, M. (2017), "An Update on Improvements in Schooling Outcomes in South Africa", *forthcoming*.

Ilifa Labantwana, Children's Insitute and DPME (2016), *South African Early Childhood Review 2016*, Ilifa Labantwana, Cape Town.

INSEAD (2016), *The Global Talent Competitiveness Index 2017*, Fontainebleau, France.

Murtin, F. (2013), "Improving Education Quality in South Africa", *OECD Economics Department Working Papers*, No. 1056, OECD Publishing, Paris.

OECD (2017), *Getting Skills Right: Financial Incentives for Steering Education and Training Acquisition*, OECD Publishing, Paris, http://dx.doi.org/10.1787/9789264272415-5-en.

OECD (2016), *Getting Skills Right: Assessing and Anticipating Changing Skill Needs*, OECD Publishing, Paris, http://dx.doi.org/10.1787/9789264252073-en.

OECD (2011), "The Impact of the 1999 Education Reform in Poland", *OECD Education Working Papers*, No. 49, OECD Publishing, Paris, http://dx.doi.org/10.1787/5kmbjgkm1m9x-en.

OECD (2010), *Recognising Non-Formal and Informal Learning: Outcomes, Policies and Practices*, OECD Publishing, Paris, http://dx.doi.org/10.1787/9789264063853-en.

Reddy, V. et al. (2016), *Skills Supply and Demand in South Africa*, LMIP Publication, Human Sciences Research Council, Pretoria.

Tan, H. and G. Lopez Acevedo (2005), "Evaluation Training Programmes for Small and Medium Enterprises: Lessons from Mexico", *World Bank Policy Research Paper*, No. 3760.

van Broekhuizen, H. (2016), "Graduate Unemployment and Higher Education Institutions in South Africa", *Stellenbosch Economic Working Papers*, No. 08/16.

van Broekhuizen, H., S. Van Der Berg and H. Hofmeyr (2016), "Higher Education Access and Outcomes for the 2008 National Matric Cohort", *Stellenbosch Economic Working Papers*, No. 16/16.

World Bank (2010), "Successful Education Reforms: Lessons from Poland", *World Bank Knowledge Brief*, Vol. 34.

Zawistowska, A. (2014), "The Black Box of the Educational Reforms in Poland: What Caused the Improvement in the PISA Scores of Polish Students", *Polish Sociological Review*, No. 3.

Database references

OECD Education Database, http://www.oecd.org/education/database.htm.

ORGANISATION FOR ECONOMIC CO-OPERATION AND DEVELOPMENT

The OECD is a unique forum where governments work together to address the economic, social and environmental challenges of globalisation. The OECD is also at the forefront of efforts to understand and to help governments respond to new developments and concerns, such as corporate governance, the information economy and the challenges of an ageing population. The Organisation provides a setting where governments can compare policy experiences, seek answers to common problems, identify good practice and work to co-ordinate domestic and international policies.

The OECD member countries are: Australia, Austria, Belgium, Canada, Chile, the Czech Republic, Denmark, Estonia, Finland, France, Germany, Greece, Hungary, Iceland, Ireland, Israel, Italy, Japan, Korea, Latvia, Luxembourg, Mexico, the Netherlands, New Zealand, Norway, Poland, Portugal, the Slovak Republic, Slovenia, Spain, Sweden, Switzerland, Turkey, the United Kingdom and the United States. The European Union takes part in the work of the OECD.

OECD Publishing disseminates widely the results of the Organisation's statistics gathering and research on economic, social and environmental issues, as well as the conventions, guidelines and standards agreed by its members.

OECD PUBLISHING, 2, rue André-Pascal, 75775 PARIS CEDEX 16
(81 2017 15 1 P) ISBN 978-92-64-27873-8 – 2017